CRYSTALS
FOR LOVE & RELATIONSHIPS

THIS IS A CARLTON BOOK

Published in 2013 by Carlton Books Limited
20 Mortimer Street
London W1T 3JW

Originally published in 2010 as part of *The New Crystal Bible*

10 9 8 7 6 5 4 3 2 1

Text © Carlton Books Ltd 2010, 2013
Design © Carlton Books Ltd 2013

A CIP catalogue record for this book is available from the British Library.

ISBN 978 1 78097 452 1

Printed in China

Disclaimer

The author and publisher shall have no liability or responsibility to any person or entity regarding any loss or damage incurred, or alleged to have incurred, directly or indirectly, by the information contained in this book.   The information provided in this book is designed to provide helpful information on the subjects discussed. This book is not meant to be used, nor should it be used, to diagnose or treat any medical condition. For diagnosis or treatment of any medical problem, consult your own physician. The publisher and author are not responsible for any specific health or allergy needs that may require medical supervision and are not liable for any damages or negative consequences from any treatment, action, application or preparation, to any person reading or following the information in this book.

CRYSTALS
FOR LOVE & RELATIONSHIPS

Your guide to 100 crystals
and their mystic powers

Cassandra Eason

CARLTON
BOOKS

Contents

INTRODUCTION

A book on crystals and gems is like no other book, because it gives access to the fabulous world of nature's most beautiful treasures. Even if you are not a crystal collector, some crystals in the book you may know already or possess as jewellery. Of the 100 minerals in the book, some are relatively rare but are quite magical, while other crystals are not externally dazzling but nevertheless contain healing or restorative properties and become valued like old friends.

Many gems and crystals have acquired myths to explain their perceived properties. Sunstone, the ancients believed, once formed part of the sun and fell to earth during a full solar eclipse. Pearls are said to be tears that fell into the ocean into open oyster shells, the tears of the angels over the sins or sorrows of humankind. This book explains, for each crystal, traditional uses for aiding physical and emotional healing, and also how they can be used practically in the home and to give personal power and protection.

A few of the rarer crystals in their natural form need to be handled carefully because they contain sulphur, lead or other potentially harmful minerals if ingested, but these I have listed. These should be displayed safely away from children or carried wrapped in a small bag.

The book does open the door to the world of wonderful minerals and you may wish to collect your favourites or wear them as jewellery. Even if you do not consider it possible that they have healing powers (and you may change you mind if you try), crystals act as a psychological boost to your energies and self-confidence or give out "do not mess with me" energies that cause others to treat you with more respect. For every crystal works in interaction with the energy field of the user or wearer and so enriches your world every time you use it.

INTRODUCING CRYSTALS

All minerals growing within the Earth have powerful energies, containing the stored natural elemental powers of their formation over millions of years, shaped by volcanic heat and waters seeping deep into the ground. Some, like black obsidian, are not crystals at all but natural glass generated by the sudden cooling of volcano-cascaded lava. Grey or fawn tubes of fulgurite are formed instantly as lightning hits sand. Others are organic, such as pearls, or made of fossils or, like golden amber, from fossilized tree resin, often containing insects or plant material. Green olivine sometimes has extra-terrestrial origins when found in stony and stony iron meteorites.

How a crystal or gem is cut can bring out its true nature. The lustrous moving cat's-eye formation that appears in such gems as yellow chrysoberyl or green alexandrite needs to be skilfully cut into dome-shaped cabochons to display its effect. So do gems that contain a six- or twelve-rayed star, like ruby or sapphire or flash opal with its appearing and disappearing flickers of rainbow colour.

Jewellery is one of the most popular ways to display gems and crystals, and benefit from their healing and empowering qualities directly through skin contact. Traditionally, earrings protect the mind from psychological attack; necklaces and pendants shield the heart from emotional manipulation and bring love; bracelets or arm bands reach out to attract abundance and opportunities. Belt buckles guard and empower the Solar Plexus and Sacral energy centres of the body that control will-power, self-confidence, needs and desires. Rings on any finger symbolize lasting love, friendship and health continuing in a never-ending cycle.

Anniversary stones and birthstones are ways of using polished and often faceted gems as tokens of deep affection or, if bought for oneself, of self-value, and are invariably luck-attracting. Tumbled or tumblestones are a relatively inexpensive way to collect a variety of stones and can be used as worry stones, displayed around the home or cast for divination. Geodes of purple amethyst or yellow citrine with numerous tiny, glittering crystals packed inside are natural ornaments, as are large pieces of dendritic limestone as nature's own unique abstract paintings. Carvings of animals or statues appear in many different stones, from creamy soapstone to deep green verdite, and act as power symbols of qualities we wish to attract, such as the courage of the lion or the focus of the hawk.

How crystals work

Many people find they are instinctively drawn to a particular rock, crystal or gemstone. Some discover that they can physically feel the crystal vibrating with energy; a tingling sensation is experienced whilst holding it. Others find that a crystal or combination of crystals makes them feel better or assists the healing of an ailment. This could be the result to some degree of the placebo effect, the mind and the power of positive thinking healing the body. Alternatively, it could be possible that the crystal's energy vibration is having a physical effect on our bodies, balancing and realigning atoms within our own bodily make-up. Whatever the answer, and there are undoubtedly many more theories, we do know that thousands of years of history show a proven and undeniable track record of the powerful properties of crystals.

What do the scientists tell us?

Solids (as well as gas and liquid) are made up of atoms, molecules and/or ions. These particles possess energy. They move in all three states – gas, liquid or solid – but differently. In gas they freely and randomly move about and have no particular connection with other particles, and have no regular form. In liquid they are more compressed; they have a "relationship" with neighbouring particles, but still have a certain amount of freedom and space to move about easily – this gives liquid its "flow". Solids are made of particles that are closely compacted together in a regular formation. However, they do have a small amount of space around them, not enough to push or shove past a neighbouring particle, but just enough to allow for a tiny amount of movement, which can cause a vibration, albeit imperceptible to the average human being. Crystals do vibrate, as can all solids.

We all know that quartz has been used to power wristwatches. Quartz is piezoelectric. This means it is capable of generating an electrical charge when under stress. Quartz is commonly used today as a crystal oscillator – an electronic circuit utilizing the mechanical resonance of a vibrating piezoelectric crystal. So, we now know that crystals, at least some of them, have a definite measurable energy.

The huge energy input in the creation of crystals transforms into power for spirituality and healing. Deep within the earth's surface the melting pot of the unknown gives rise to crystals of immense beauty and powerful grounding energies. A collision of material from outer space leaves us its rare and wonderful offspring.

Holding one of these gifts of nature, allowing it to resonate with our own energies and letting it assist us in our healing efforts, whether for our own benefit or to heal another, suggests that crystals have powers, even if these simply mean triggering our own inner healing abilities.

The art of using crystals in healing has developed over many centuries. One day, science may be able to give us a definitive answer as to how and why they work as an aid to healing. Thousands, if not millions, of people have enjoyed the healing benefits of crystals over the centuries and continue to do so today. If they did not work, people would not continue to use them; perhaps this is a good enough reason to believe in what may seem to sceptics to be unbelievable

CRYSTAL SHAPES AND TERMS

To identify crystals, we look at their mineral content and their structure. Crystals form in a variety of ways and their resulting structures or "habits" can be grouped into six (or sometimes seven) groups or "systems". Crystals are grouped based on the symmetry (or lack of it) of their three-dimensional structures:

Cubic or isometric

This is the simplest and one of the most common crystal forms, where its three axes meet at 90° angles and all are the same length. There are six faces in parallel pairs. This crystal formation has total symmetry. Within the isometric system however, there are 14 more formations, increasing in complexity, built upon this simple structure, for example the dodecahedron and octahedron.
Examples: diamond, garnet and halite, among many others.

Tetragonal

Similar to the cubic (or isometric) system, this has three axes that are at a 90° angle to each other. However, whilst the two horizontal axes are of the same length, the vertical axis is either longer or shorter. Again, there are various formations based on this system, many of which, to the untrained eye, have little resemblance to the simple shape illustrated here.
Examples: scapolite, vesuvianite and zircon.

Hexagonal

In this system there is an additional axis, which gives the crystal six sides. The three horizontal axes meet at 60° angles to each other and the vertical axis is at a 90° angle to the horizontal axes. Included in the hexagonal system is a sub-system called the trigonal system.
Examples of hexagonal: aquamarine, beryl, emerald and zincite.
Examples of trigonal: quartz, ruby, sapphire and tiger's eye.

Orthorhombic

Here, like the isometric system, the three axes meet at a 90° angle to each other, but they are all different lengths.
Examples: chrysoberyl, peridot, sulphur and topaz.

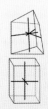

Monoclinic

In this system all the axes have different lengths as with the orthorhombic system, but with two sides perpendicular and the base at an angle, forming a parallelogram.
Examples: azurite, gypsum, jadeite and malachite.

Triclinic

This crystal system has no symmetry. All axes are different lengths and there are no axial angles of 90°.
Examples: kyanite, labradorite, oligoclase and turquoise.

Finally we have amorphous materials. These are not minerals. They are non-crystalline materials but are usually included within the general subject of crystals and gems. Formed by a variety of natural processes such as volcanic activity or fossilization, they include amber, glass, jet, obsidian and opal.

CRYSTALS AND COLOURS

The colour of a crystal is the most important and easiest way of identifying the right one. If a colour is hot like red, associated with life blood and fire, its action will be fast. In contrast, a green crystal represents gradual growth and nature. The shade of a crystal also offers clues: sparkling transparent clear quartz, reflecting sunlight, has different energies from cloudier shimmering white selenite that resembles moonlight. You can enhance the power of a crystal by burning a candle of a similar colour. It is a good idea to build up a collection of crystals in different shades and intensity of brightness. You can also use an antidote colour, for example a blue crystal if someone is very angry or a situation is too fast moving. The following are traditional colour associations.

White colourless

Originality, beginnings, clarity, inspiration, developing talents, ambitions, breaking bad luck, good health, vitality, spiritual development, contact with angels and spirit guides. Can be substituted for any other colour.
Healing powers: May help whole-body healing, general health, integration of mind, body and soul, brain, neurological disorders, auto-immune system, pain relief. **Antidote:** Grey.

White cloudy
(translucent) or opaque (solid colour)

Nurturing, slower new beginnings, especially after loss, slower unfolding potential, protection against negativity, mothers and babies, hope, granting wishes and fulfilling dreams, calling love from the past or afar.
Healing powers: Believed to assist with hormones, fluid balance, fertility, pregnancy, recovery from illness, depression or exhaustion, bone marrow, cells. **Antidote:** Yellow.

Red

Courage, positive change, strength, determination, power, sexual passion, male potency, initiative, competitiveness, protecting loved ones, survival, overcoming obstacles.
Healing powers: Claimed to help improve energy, muscles, low blood pressure, circulation, blood ailments, feet, hands, skeleton, reproductive organs, lifts depression. **Antidote:** Blue.

Orange

Confidence, joy, creativity, female fertility (also red), abundance, independence, self-esteem.
Healing powers: Thought to be good for ovaries, intestines, increases pulse rate, kidneys, bladder, menstruation, menopause, food allergies and addictions, arthritis, rheumatism, immune system **Antidote:** Indigo.

Yellow

Logic, memory, determination, tests, technology, job changes, communication, money-making, short-distance moves and holidays, conventional healing, surgery, repelling malice.
Healing powers: Melp help the lymphatic system, metabolism, blood sugar (also green and blue), digestion, liver, gall bladder, pancreas, spleen, nervous system, eczema, skin problems, nausea, sickness. **Antidote:** Violet.

Green

Love, commitment, beauty, environment, healing via nature, crystal healing, gradual increase of health, wealth, luck.
Healing powers: Thought to be beneficial for heart, lungs, respiratory system, infections and viruses, high blood pressure (also blue), pollen and fur allergies, addictions and obsessions (also blue). **Antidote:** None needed.

Blue
Idealism, justice, career, authority, long-distance travel and house moves, marriage, partnerships, prosperity, peace.
Healing powers: Believed to help thyroid gland, throat, fevers, teeth, cuts, inflammation, childhood rashes, bruises, burns, high blood pressure, eyesight, communication disorders. **Antidote:** Red.

Purple
Spirituality, imagination, dreams, psychic powers, intuition, teaching, counselling, healing from higher sources, banishing past sorrow or present troublesome influences.
Healing powers: Claimed to help with headaches, migraines, scalp, ears, hair, sinusitis, childbirth, addictions, neuroses, phobias, nerve endings and connections, allergies to chemicals and modern living, hyperactivity, insomnia. **Antidote:** Orange.

Pink
Reconciliation, happy family relationships, friendship, kindness, children and teenagers, girls entering puberty, young or new love and trust after betrayal.
Healing powers: Believed to assist with glands, ears, stress headaches, PMS, skin, ulcers, psychosomatic and stress-induced ills, insomnia, nightmares, family ills, children, abuse and self hatred **Antidote:** Dark blue.

Brown
Practical matters, security, accumulation of money, learning new skills in later years, property, finding what is lost, perseverance.
Healing powers: Claimed to be helpful for feet, legs, bowels, hernia, anus, prostate, chronic conditions, growths, degenerative conditons in old age, panic. **Antidote:** Green.

Grey
Adaptability, neutralizing unfriendly energies, peace-making, keeping secrets, shielding from psychic attack.
Healing powers: May help to ease tesions, wounds, burns, tissue and nerve connections, obsessions and acute anxiety, persistent pain. **Antidote:** Clear white.

Gold
Protection, fulfilling ambitions, large infusion of money and resources, long life, recognition, recovery after setbacks, healing when prognosis is not good.
Healing powers: Believed to be beneficial for nervous system, spine, skin, addictions, obsessions and compulsions, minor miracles, healing whole system. **Antidote:** None needed.

Silver
Establishing natural fertility cycles, luck, truth, intuition, female spirituality, unexpected money, attracting love.
Healing powers: May help cleanse toxins, visual disturbances, epilepsy, nightmares, eases passing of a loved one.
Antidote: None needed.

Black
Transformation, peaceful endings, grief, banishing sorrow, guilt and destructive influences, acceptance, blocking a negative force, psychic protection.
Healing powers: Said to assist with pain relief, constipation, IBS, side effects of invasive treatments.
Antidote: Clear white.

CHOOSING & CLEANSING CRYSTALS

Our ancestors looked on hillsides or seashores to find their crystals, and it is still possible to find beautiful stones in nature. Working with crystals local to your area is especially powerful, however, in the modern world there is a huge array of beautifully polished crystals obtainable by anyone. If you want to collect crystals there is no substitute for visiting a specialist crystal store and passing your hand over a tray of similar crystals to feel the one that is right for you. Equally, handling a series of crystal pendulums or gazing within different spheres will reveal which is your special crystal.

At a mineral store, too, you can receive advice about the composition of crystals. Museums with a geological section are usually a good place to buy high-quality mineral specimens. You can also buy crystals by mail order using the images on the Internet site as a guide. Run your hand in front of the screen or over a printout until you feel your palm tingling.

With crystals, size is not important: what matters is the composition of the crystal. Nor should you feel that you need spend a fortune. It is better to buy, for example, a small piece of natural citrine rather than a much larger, heat-treated specimen. Likewise, less colourful stones are preferable to ones that have been dyed. If in doubt check with images on a mineralogical site to see the raw product.

There are a number of ways you can cleanse crystals when you first acquire them, before and after a healing session or if you are using a crystal for good luck or protection. Some methods take a minute or two, but use one of the slower acting techniques at least monthly. If your crystals appear dull or feel heavier than usual they may need extra cleansing.

Water

Wash crystals under a running tap. This works for most tumblestones except those that are fragile or metallic but not for gems. Lapis lazuli and turquoise can be damaged by prolonged water contact. Leave crystals to dry naturally or use a soft cloth kept only for your crystals.

Amethyst geodes

You only need a small amethyst geode (clusters of tiny amethysts embedded in a piece of rock). Stand individual crystals or points on the flat part of the geode. Alternatively make a circle of crystals around a large unpolished amethyst.

The cleansing will take 24 hours. Citrine can be kept with crystals to keep it fresh between more formal cleansing.

Using Mother Earth

Burying crystals in soil for 24 hours is a good way of resting an overworked crystal and is especially effective for crystal points. Choose a deep indoor or outdoor plant pot with a growing plant such as lavender, rose or rosemary or sage herbs. This works best for unpolished natural stones. For a delicate crystal, rest it on top of the soil in an open dish.

Using fragrance

This is suitable for any crystal or gem. Circle a sagebrush or cedar smudge stick or a lemon-grass, pine, juniper, frankincense, lavender or rose incense stick in anti-clockwise spirals over any crystals to be cleansed for three or four minutes. Leave the incense to burn through near the crystals.

Using sound

Collect any crystals to be purified and over them ring either a hand bell or Tibetan bells nine times or strike a small singing bowl over them for about a minute until the sound ceases. Repeat twice more. Sound is an efficient cleanser if you have been working with any intense sorrow or healing when the official medical prognosis of the patient is not good.

Light

Sunlight is the best cleanser for vibrant, richly coloured or sparkling crystals. Leave the crystals from dawn till noon. If the day is cloudy substitute a small gold-coloured or natural beeswax candle for sunlight and leave your crystals in a circle round the candle in a safe place until the candle burns through or goes out naturally. Aventurine, amethyst, aquamarine, beryl, citrine, fluorite and rose quartz do not respond well to sunlight. Crystals in transparent or translucent softer shades or that have clouds or inclusions tend to do better in moonlight, and rose quartz and amethyst are very responsive to lunar energies. The night of the full moon is best for cleansing. Leave all your crystals if possible in a sheltered place outdoors or on an indoor window ledge every month all night on full moon night or a night leading up to the full moon.

Salt

Salt is abrasive and can damage crystals so don't soak the crystals in salt but make three clockwise circles of salt around the crystals. Leave the crystals within the salt circles for about 12 hours, any time of the day or evening and night. Then scoop up the salt from the circles and dissolve it in water. Tip the salt water away under a running tap. Alternatively rest the crystals in a dish on top of a large bowl of salt for 12 hours.

Infusions

This is a very traditional method. Sprinkle a crystal with a few drops of hyssop or rosemary infusion and then wipe it clean with a cloth. To make the infusion, add a teaspoon of dried hyssop or rosemary herb to a cup of boiling water, stir, cover, leave for ten minutes, then strain. Alternatively, use amethyst elixir: soak an amethyst in cold water for a few hours then remove the amethyst. If working with a gem or delicate crystal, sprinkle the infusion round the crystal in circles or float it in a small sealed container in the water or infusion overnight. Dried herbs, particularly sage, thyme, rosemary and hyssop, are excellent cleansers and you can place a delicate crystal or gem in a dish in a larger bowl of herbs for 12 hours.

USING CRYSTALS IN YOUR LIFE

Although crystals are often associated with healing, they are useful in every aspect of daily life. In each individual crystal entry I have listed everyday purposes and how a crystal can be helpful for spiritual or psychic development. The power of crystals involves both psychology and something less definable in the interaction of crystal with user. If we feel confident and powerful or beautiful, then that is the impression we give and so we attract positive reactions that reinforce the new, more open behaviour.

Crystals can be used to improve all kinds of relationships, whether you are hoping to attract your soul mate, address problems in an existing partnership, reconnect with an old friend or want some guidance on dealing with a child. As part of your quest to develop relationships, you may want to use your crystals for fortune telling. People have been using crystals for divination for thousands of years as it was believed that crystals could provide access to information about the future from deities, angels and spirits. In the modern world we use crystal spheres, eggs, pendulums and small crystals to access our own inner wisdom and use our innate clairvoyant powers to see not a fixed future but the possibilities that may result from our taking particular actions. The images we see within or on the surface of crystals are projected by our inner or psychic eye into the crystal, so that we may actually physically see them, though they may be symbolic. However, some people only ever see images in their mind, but with great accuracy stimulated by the reflective surface of the crystal. Clairvoyant vision that is central to scrying, the word used for seeing or sensing images on or within reflective surfaces such as crystals, is not restricted by the limits of the physical eye range, and so using crystals we can see distant places or people far away or beings from other dimensions by a process called remote viewing. Claivoyance also enables us to look into past worlds and past lives that may hold clues to present dilemmas, as well as forwards to the future not yet made.

CRYSTALS TO USE FOR LOVE

Love crystals work by opening our personal energy field or aura to attract and to keep love in our lives and encourage fidelity. They can make a relationship more resistant to outside influences that may seek to come between a couple or family, and help to keep a couple together when times get hard. They also act as a bond and reminder of what was good, if problems cause a temporary parting or one of the partners to be unfaithful.

Soft pink crystals like rose quartz are excellent for new love, particularly after a former breakdown in trust, while deeper green crystals such as jade or emerald represent fidelity. Strong deep red gems, like garnet or ruby, bring love that endures in good times and bad. Gems such as sapphires and diamonds form traditional pledges of love and are often given as rings at a time of betrothal or major commitment.

Copper, the metal of Venus, goddess of love, as well as the more usual silver, the romantic metal of the moon, and gold, signifying love forever belonging to the sun, are also exchanged as relationship rings. Rare platinum is the ultimate twin-soul, "our love will last forever and a day" metal.

Orange crystals like carnelian are fertility and potency symbols and, as with moonstone or selenite, are linked with conceiving an infant.

Love crystals include:

Amber (orange): Protects against negative outside influences and interference; calls a twin soul.

Amethyst (purple): Heals love quarrels, removing obsessions or addictions by one partner that cause problems in the relationship.

Angelite (blue): Reduces anger in a partner or unnecessary quarrels if both of you have strong opinions; also encourages spiritual love.

Aquamarine (pale blue): Calls a lover back; helps two people with different lifestyles to live together in harmony, reduces the effects of sensitive issues that cause quarrels.

Carnelian (orange and red): Rekindles passion that has faded in an otherwise loving relationship; for the consummation of love. (See pages 35 and 40).

Chrysoprase (green): Opens you to new love, for overcoming a period of stagnation or a sticking point in a relationship. (See page 111).

Jade (green): The crystal of new love, gentle love and fidelity and love in later life: increases trustworthiness in love. (See page 97).

Jasper (red): Passion helps a woman to overcome a jealous love rival or unfair opposition to a relationship. (See page 31).

Jet (black): Overcomes sorrow for lost love and broken relationships so that you can start again. (See page 72).

Moonstone (cream and shimmering): First or new love and the increase of passion; good if love must be kept a secret. (See page 54).

Moss agate (deep green with pale blue or white inclusions): The gradual increase of love and commitment, love growing from friendship or with a work colleague.

Rose quartz (pink): To attract gentle love and romance or to call a lover to you.

ANNIVERSARY GEM STONES

Official list of the American Gem Trade Association

1st	Gold	12th	Jade	23rd	Imperial topaz
2nd	Garnet	13th	Citrine	24th	Tanzanite
3rd	Cultured or natural pearls	14th	Opal	25th	Silver (top right)
4th	Blue topaz	15th	Ruby (top left)	30th	Cultured or natural pearl
5th	Sapphire	16th	Peridot (top middle)	35th	Emerald
6th	Amethyst	17th	Carnelian or watches	40th	Ruby
7th	Onyx	18th	Cat's eye	45th	Sapphire (bottom right)
8th	Tourmaline	19th	Aquamarine	50th	Gold
9th	Lapis lazuli	20th	Emerald	55th	Alexandrite (bottom left)
10th	Diamond	21st	Iolite	60th	Diamond
11th	Turquoise	22nd	Spinel		

Making a crystal elixir

What are crystal elixirs?

Crystal-infused elixirs are empowered water that has been filled with the spiritual energy of crystals by soaking a crystal in the water. The infused water acts as a vehicle for vibrations of the crystal which interacts with the person's own energy field.

Making crystal elixirs - direct infusion method

· A rounded tumbled crystal the size of an average coin will infuse a normal-sized glass or bottle of water. However, you can add two crystals, either of the same kind or with different properties, to quantities of water up to 500 or 600ml.

· Work with three small crystals, the same kind or mixed, for up to 100ml. Increase the number of crystals proportionately if you want even bigger quantities.

· Wash the crystal/s under running water.

· Place the crystal/s in the water using tongs. Still mineral or distilled/filtered water is good; tap water is fine for animals, plants and around the home or your workspace.

· Cover the container or put the lid back on.

· Hold the sealed container between your hands, stating the purpose of the elixir. Ask that the elixir be "created for the greatest good and purest purpose to bring the healing/help/protection in the way that is right for the person/circumstances".

· Leave the water and crystal/s in the refrigerator overnight.

· Unless you have made a glass of crystal elixir to drink immediately, pour the water into suitable containers when you wake.

· Remove the crystal/s.

Crystal waters keep their full power for about 24 hours or three days in the refrigerator.

Indirect crystal elixir

Use this method for a very concentrated elixir with a larger number of the same crystal (up to seven crystals) or crystals with complementary powers, for extra protection, healing or if results seem slow. It is also a suitable method to use with one or two crystals if you are concerned about soaking them directly in drinking water; also for safe elixirs with porous, natural (not tumblestones) or delicate crystals or gemstones, but not for toxic ones (see below).

· Half fill a large glass bowl.

· Hold the crystal/s or gem/s in your cupped hands over the water and stating the purpose of the elixir as in method 1.

· Place the crystal/s or gem/s in a small, fully sealable glass container.

· Close the lid and float the small container in the water in the bowl.

· Cover the bowl or put fine mesh across so it cannot become polluted.

· Leave the bowl for a full 24-hour cycle indoors near a window. Fill bottles with the water and use as needed.

Warning

For crystals listed as toxic, the only safe way to make elixirs is placing a glass or jug of water near a toxic crystal in a sealed container for 48 hours. Make sure the crystal does not come into contact with water or glass.

CREATING A CRYSTAL LAYOUT

By using crystals arranged in a regular geometric formation, called a healing grid or layout, you can concentrate and focus healing energies in a way that is more powerful than working with separate crystals. You can work with as few as three crystals or use as many as you wish to create radiating stars or wheels with lines of crystals. The crystals need only be small.

Using round crystals

You will need one set of six rose quartz or purple amethyst crystals for bringing calm and removing pain and illness. Also a second set of either six yellow citrines or clear quartz crystals for energizing and health-restoring. For removing illness and energizing at the same time alternate three energizers with three calming pain-removers. Arrange the crystals, one over the head and one under the feet as the patient lies down, and the others evenly on either side, a few centimetres away from the body. Add or substitute crystals from the problems list. For extra power, place an additional crystal on the body just above the navel. This should be a crystal related to the main problem.

Crystal points and crystal grids

For more dynamic, faster healing, you can create your layout from six or eight crystal points. Again, set a round crystal related to the problem in the centre on the body. In a crystal layout, set the point facing outwards to remove any illness, sorrow, addictions, blockages or pain and pointing inwards to energize and to bring healing. Alternatively, position the points so every other one faces outwards to bring balanced energies. Double-terminated crystals, with a point at both ends, ensure a two-way energy flow. For the simplest procedure, having set up the layout and asked the blessings of angels and guides, sit

or lie within the crystal grid for between 15 and 20 minutes and let nature do its work. Afterwards remove the crystals one by one in reverse order of setting.

The Master crystal

For additional power, join together the individual crystals with what is called a master crystal. In direct healing, this is usually a pointed, thin, clear wand-like crystal. Touch each crystal with the master crystal wand once you have set the crystal in its grid position and then draw visualized lines of light between the crystals moving clockwise to join them to each other. Join these visualized lines of light as if you were drawing them physically, starting and finishing at the highest point over the head and then go round a second or even third time until you feel the vibrating humming connection of the crystals. Finally, touch the central crystal with the wand and picture straight rays of pulsating light radiating from it connecting it to every other crystal. For absent healing, if using a photo, you can set a larger master crystal cluster in the centre and visualize the rays of light forming a wheel with the central crystal as the hub, radiating out to each of the individual crystals.

Healing with a layout

You or the person to be healed should lie flat with the head slightly propped up. For a shorter treatment, arrange the crystals around a chair and ask the patient to hold the central crystal or set it under the middle of the chair. If the grid is on the floor, kneel to join the crystals with the visualized light rays using your wand. If the layout is round yourself you can create the shape in light over your head with the master wand as you visualize the figure of light expanding to enclose you.

THE CRYSTAL TAROT

Choosing crystal substitutes for the 22 major tarot cards combines the living energy of associated crystals with the traditional meaning of tarot cards. Holding each selected crystal triggers rich clairvoyant images in your mind to answer any question. This is because the crystals chosen from a drawstring bag without looking amplify your innate psychic powers, linking you to the cosmic source of hidden wisdom, past, present and future.

Tarot crystal meanings

The Fool: Clear crystal quartz.
Being true to yourself and new beginnings. Take a leap into the unknown.

The Magician: Carnelian.
Creativity, the entrepreneur. Passion; put ideas and plans into action now.

The High Priestess: Amethyst.
Healing and unique talents. Follow your own path: act independently.

The Empress: Jade.
Mothering and nurturing: care for yourself as well as others.

Emperor: Turquoise or blue howlite.
Fathering, ambitions. Be determined; take the lead.

The Hierophant: Lapis lazuli or sodalite.
Tradition, responsibility. Take the long-term view and play safe.

The Lovers: Rose quartz.
Love, romance and family: choices, reconciliation.

The Chariot: Rutilated quartz or laboradite.
Travel or chosen change: decide and steer your own destiny.

Justice: Banded agate.
Law, officialdom and injustice: stand by your principles.

The Hermit: Desert rose.
Withdrawal from conflict. Listen to your inner voice, not others.

The Wheel of Fortune: Green aventurine.
Good luck, changes in circumstance: turn challenges to opportunity.

Strength: Malachite.
Winning through difficulty; renewed energy. Persevere quietly.

The Hanged Man: Bloodstone/heliotrope.
Letting go; trust. Short-term sacrifice will bring some long-term gain.

Death: Apache tear or jet.
Endings leading to beginnings: grieve and move on. This never foretells actual death.

Temperance: Blue lace agate.
Harmony, moderation: a time to compromise.

The Devil: Red jasper.
Suppressed anger: express grievances and needs calmly.

The Tower: Leopardskin jasper or snakeskin agate.
Freedom from restrictions: temporary disruption brings liberation.

The Star: Citrine.
Recognition, achieving dreams. Develop hidden talents.

The Moon: Moonstone or selenite.
Fertility, intuition. Avoid illusion and deception.

The Sun: Amber.

Health, prosperity, happiness: life will be good.

Judgment: Hawk's eye/falcon's eye.

Criticism, guilt: accept mistakes and move forward.

The World: Aquamarine.

Relocation, long-distance travel: seize opportunities.

Reading your crystal tarot

· Place the 22 stones in a bag.

· Ask and concentrate on an issue or question.

· Put the hand you write with into the bag, touch each crystal and pull out the crystal that feels right.

· Read its tarot meaning and then hold it in cupped hands.

· Ask to be shown or told as pictures or words in your mind what is unknown to you about the circumstances surrounding the question and the true feelings of other people involved.

· Place each crystal on the table after reading it.

· Choose a second crystal to show the best action to take or change in direction needed.

· Do the same for the third crystal, asking the outcome of any action or change in direction within three months. For a longer-term outcome pick a fourth crystal for the 12 months ahead.

Spell casting with crystals

· Choose a crystal. Each crystal has its own magic meaning, carnelian for courage and confidence, amber for fertility, jade for gentle love, green aventurine for good luck.

· Use a white candle for attracting good things and a dark purple or blue one to bind or banish. If you are binding or want to remove something, you will also need a bowl of earth or sand.

· Light the candle to put the spell energies into motion and say what you seek to attract or want to remove from your life.

· Next, pass the crystal clockwise nine times in a circle above the candle flame, repeating as a short phrase what you want or do not want, three times. For instance, you could say "Bring me money soon" or "Stop (name) from bullying me".

· Toss the crystal up and down rhythmically higher and higher between your hands as you repeat the words

louder and faster and, if you wish, stamp your feet in time. For example, "Take away fear".

· When you feel that the spell power is at its height, call out "Take away fear NOW!" and give the crystal a final toss higher in the air.

· As fast as possible, blow out the candle still holding the crystal to attract your wish.

· To bind or banish something or someone, do not blow out the candle straight away but very rapidly transfer the crystal to the hand you do not write with.

· Push the flame end of the candle into a bowl of earth with the hand you write with.

· Carry the crystal as a symbol of what you wish to attract in the days ahead and repeat the closing words nine times in your mind, picturing the successful outcome.

· For binding and banishing, bury the crystal immediately after the spell. Alternatively, for banishing throw the crystal into running water or for binding keep it in a small lidded container in the coldest part of the freezer.

THE CRYSTAL DIRECTORY

The 100 crystals are listed according to colour so that you can easily find ones for particular purposes. Colour is a good indication of the basic nature of the crystal. For example red crystals and gems tend to be far more dynamic in their energies and faster acting than more reflective purple ones. But within the colour groupings there are variations that partly depend on the chemical composition and partly on the shade or vibrancy of the individual crystal.

Each entry is divided into categories so you can check its individual properties, beginning with the kind of crystal it is and its physical and emotional healing properties. There are also listings for everyday uses and magical significance. Also included is which chakra the crystal corresponds with. Every crystal is related to one of seven energy centres in the body known as chakras. Each chakra controls different parts of the body and mind and the energy channels that link them. To feel your chakras, hold the palm of the hand you do not write with over each area. If the chakra is in balance, you will sense a warm, swirling sensation. If it feels jarring or unpleasant, the chakra is probably overactive. If you feel nothing, it may be blocked. To heal blocked or overactive chakras, use small round or oval chakra crystals and hold the appropriate crystal in turn over the relevant area. The body will take the required amount of healing. If any chakra us particularly blocked or in overdrive, you can give it extra input. To perform chakra touch healing, choose a crystal for each chakra and hold it in the hand you do not write with. Ask for blessings and guidance from the angels and guides and hold each crystal over the appropriate chakra area. Gently massage the chakra to slow it down or unblock it. When you sense the energies are in balance, continue with the next crystal until you have used all seven. Pass your hands down the sides of the body a few centimetres away from it to smooth the energies of the aura field surrounding the body then cleanse your crystals.

The sign of the zodiac associated with the crystal is given as you may find your personal star sign crystals are particularly lucky or empowering. The divinatory meaning explains the essential quality of the crystal. Finally, a short section of information describes what makes that crystal unique and also sometimes the myths and beliefs that have grown up around it to explain those special qualities.

STRAWBERRY QUARTZ

Type: Silicon dioxide, quartz, often mottled in its natural form. Clear strawberry quartz is artificially produced and is more brittle.

Colours: Natural strawberry quartz is mid pink, sometimes with lighter pink markings, but is occasionally a more translucent strawberry colour, particularly when polished.

Availability: Relatively rare.

Physical benefits: Thought to relieve skin rashes, rosacea, scars and lesions, bruises, food allergies and heart irregularities, excessive blushing and stammering.

Emotional healing: Increases self-esteem in people from over-critical families, or with a controlling partner, so making breaking out of the cycle of self-doubt easier.

Chakra: Heart.

Candle colour: *Pink.*
Fragrances: *Apple blossom, chamomile, clary sage, mimosa, strawberry.*
Practical uses: *A good stone for parents with large families to enjoy the happy special moments and not be overwhelmed by responsibility; for any family where one parent is frequently away. Take on days out, especially in summer, to experience joy.*
Magical significance: *Natural strawberry quartz is a gentle introduction to past-life work/out-of-body travel. Hold one in the hand you do not write with while listening to hypnotherapy or psychic journeying CDs.*
Divinatory meaning: *Time for self-nurturing; close the door unless someone is offering you help.*
Zodiac: *Taurus.*
Empowerment: *I need not fill every moment with activity*

A gentle, comforting crystal associated with the mother goddess. Good for children who hate being away from the home; keep a strawberry quartz with a baby's travel cot for sleeping in unfamiliar places and rub it over your young child's favourite toy to reassure them if they are staying overnight without a parent.

A bowl of strawberry quartz tumblestones makes temporary accommodation more home-like; carry one on long journeys to relax you into sleep and to make hotel rooms feel welcoming. A calming stone at home to keep a sense of perspective if others create dramas. Keep strawberry quartz near soft fruits to preserve their freshness.

Botswana Agate

Type: Chalcedony.

Colours: Pink, cream and grey bands, sometimes with an eye formation that is considered especially lucky.
Availability: Common.

Physical benefits: Thought to relieve sexual dysfunctions in both sexes; stomach problems; be good for stimulating the body's immune system; help the body to absorb oxygen so benefiting the circulation; be good for the skin; see as treating underlying causes of illness rather than the symptoms.

Emotional healing: A crystal of infinite possibility and hope, so balancing depression, fears such as agoraphobia and panic attacks, especially in crowded places; helps all who have suffered loss and still grieve; relieves emotional blocks to fertility.

Chakra: Sacral.

Candle colour: *Pink.*
Fragrances: *Cherry blossom, geranium, magnolia, peach.*
Practical uses: *Suggests practical solutions rather than dwelling on the reasons for a situation or assigning blame.*
Magical significance: *The eye formation is both protective and lucky. Hold one while choosing lucky numbers for a lottery or picking a horse for a race.*
Divinatory meaning: *You may have to look for an opportunity or solution, but it has been there all the time, hidden by looking too far away and missing the obvious.*
Zodiac: *Gemini.*
Empowerment: *I call fertility and blessings into my life.*

Named after the land in Africa where it was discovered, Botswana agate is called the sunset stone: it retains sunlight which can comfort people through dark, lonely nights. Traditionally the crystals were used in African fertility ceremonies to encourage potency and the conception of strong, healthy offspring. This crystal is ideal for children and teenagers who are sensitive and easily hurt by teasing, and will help them to find like-minded friends; good if you are joining a dating agency or embarking on online dating to find someone with whom you are spiritually in tune and who shares your dreams.

Pink Kunzite

Type: Silicate/spodumene with manganese that causes the pink colour.

Colours: Pink, striated, sometimes with streaks of white.

Availability: Relatively common.

Physical benefits: May help with hormone-linked migraines, the reproductive system in women, puberty in girls, PMS, menstrual problems, skin rashes caused by allergies to chemicals, circulation, heart, neuralgia, epilepsy, reducing the after-effects of anaesthesia.

Emotional healing: Relieves heartache and heartbreak, particularly in women; for human and animal mothers who find it hard to care for their young, for whatever reason, or who need mothering themselves; good for sleepless babies and over-active small children.

Chakra: Heart.

Kunzite was named in 1902 after New York jeweller and gemstone specialist George Frederick Kunz, who catalogued and described its properties.

Wear pink kunzite if you want to find new love after a relationship breakdown or to marry someone you love who is scared to commit to a relationship.

The colour of kunzite, like tourmaline, can vary according to the angle from which you look at it. This phenomenon is called pleochroism or multicolouredness, and in a cut stone the best colour is seen from above.

Candle colour: *Pink.*

Fragrances: *Clary sage, magnolia, mimosa, rose, violet.*

Practical uses: *Called in its pink shades the woman's stone, kunzite jewellery is an ideal gift for a girl entering puberty to help her love her changing body; for a young or first-time mother and for all single mothers, to feel supported.*

Magical significance: *Pink kunzite has been adopted by people in conventional religions and in alternative forms of spirituality to symbolize reverence for a Mother Goddess as the creatrix and nurturer of all living things.*

Divinatory meaning: *What a relative or very close friend is saying is not what they mean; ask gentle but probing questions to discover the real problem.*

Zodiac: *Pisces and Taurus.*

Empowerment: *I am sensitive to my own hidden needs.*

RHODONITE

Type: Manganese inosilicate/chain silicate.

Colours: Pink or salmon pink, usually with varying size of black patches, veins and inclusions; less frequently red or red-brown.

Availability: Common.

Physical benefits: May be useful for insect bites, stings and allergic reactions caused by them, cuts, wounds, scar tissue, birth marks, ulcers, skin conditions caused by allergies, auto-immune conditions, emphysema and other chronic or progressive lung conditions.

Emotional healing: Heals the mental scars of a violent lover; relieves the pain of unrequited love; reduces obsession for a love who would never leave an existing relationship.

Chakra: Heart.

In Feng Shui, rhodonite balances yin and yang energies. Even if you know nothing about Feng Shui, hold a rhodonite massage wand in the hand you write with and walk around the home. If energies are too yang, you will feel a surge in your finger; if too yin, the wand will feel lifeless; if energies are balanced, you will experience tranquillity. In places that are too yang, set a rhodonite that is more black than pink, and the reverse if an area feels too yin.

   As a crystal of gentle love, wear rhodonite jewellery after a break-up to learn to love yourself, to avoid dashing into the first relationship on offer and maybe repeating old mistakes.

Candle colour: *Rose pink.*
Fragrances: *Geranium, hyacinth, magnolia, narcissus, rose.*
Practical uses: *Keep rhodonite where you relax, to calm those who have trouble controlling their temper, swear or argue; put one by your computer to protect family members online.*
Magical significance: *Rhodonite transmits positive energies to service personnel, peacekeepers, aid workers and those in war zones. Set a dish of tumbled rhodonites or a rhodonite egg next to a picture of a war-torn area or a loved one serving overseas. Light a rose-pink candle and name those you wish to bless.*
Divinatory meaning: *Examine your innermost emotions to determine what you really want to be and who, if anyone, you want to be with.*
Zodiac: *Aries.*
Empowerment: *Love is stronger than anger.*

Halite/Rock Salt

Type: Halide/sodium chloride.

Colours: Pink, white or colourless (the pure form); also orange, yellow and red.

Availability: Common.

Physical benefits: Can help lungs, allergies that cause respiratory problems, sinus, migraines, infections, absorption of necessary minerals, colon and lower intestinal tract disorders, water retention, chemical imbalances in the body or mind.

Emotional healing: Pink halite heals emotional problems connected with relationships, especially those where past ties and responsibilities that still exist prevent a totally fresh start.

Chakra: Heart and Sacral.

Halite, isometric crystals formed after the evaporation of briny waters from seas or salt lakes, is a fast-growing crystal; some specimens sold can be less than a year old. It can also, however, be found as deposits in ancient bedrock where once, long, long ago, there were seas or salt lakes.

Pink halite is a crystal for surviving setbacks and starting over again, whether in a relationship, a new love or a new location, so that you can build on past knowledge. Halite also lifts the bad moods of others.

Candle colour: *Pink.*
Fragrances: *Acacia, anise, eucalyptus, rose, tea tree.*
Practical uses: *Halite is often carved into lamps, used as natural air ionizers to improve air quality. It benefits anyone with pet allergies, hay fever or asthma, reduces emissions from electrical items and induces health and well-being.*
Magical significance: *Leave a small piece of white halite to dissolve undisturbed in cold water; then put a little of the solution to dry out in a warm place; concave or hopper crystals gradually form; pour the rest away under running water to increase the flow of good luck and prosperity.*
Divinatory meaning: *You may be tempted to abandon a situation but it is better to build on the good aspects.*
Zodiac: *Cancer and Pisces.*
Empowerment: *I value and preserve what I have built up.*

STILBITE

Type: Zeolite, tectosilicate, belonging to the zoisite family.

Colours: Pink, creamy pink, peach, white.
Availability: Relatively common in clusters, rarer as tumblestones.

Physical benefits: Thought to be helpful to rid the system of toxins, for laryngitis, sun burn, melanomas, skin pigmentation problems, torn or strained ligaments, bad reaction to prescription drugs.

Emotional healing: Gentle healing of all emotional issues, particularly those connected with a relationship breakdown when a partner walked out or the death or disappearance of a parent, especially the mother.

Chakra: Heart, Throat and Crown.

Stilbite is often found joined to apophyllite crystals. When it is teamed up with any other crystals, it amplifies their energies and is itself increased in healing powers. If you are new to pursuing psychic development, stilbite guides the subconscious mind to higher realms, where deep insights and intuitive thoughts can be accessed. Place by your child's bedside when you tell a bedtime story to gather loving energies together if you have been working late.

Candle colour: *Pink or white.*
Fragrances: *Geranium, honeysuckle.*
Practical uses: *Place under a pillow or near your bed to help with sleep problems, helpful if you suffer frequent nightmares.*
Magical significance: *Focus on this crystal by the light of a geranium-scented candle to achieve communication with your guardian angel.*
Divinatory meaning: *A period of creativity is indicated that may involve loved ones, working on a long desired and overdue home improvement.*
Zodiac: *Aries and Taurus.*
Empowerment: *I am filled with love for life.*

PINK TOPAZ

Type: Fluorine aluminium silicate; occurs naturally but many pink topaz are dyed.

Colours: From pale to brighter or reddish pink.

Availability: Rare in untreated form.

Physical benefits: Thought to reduce toxins in body, breasts and ovaries; may help with early-onset puberty, menopause, HRT treatment, inflammation, burns and fevers, fertility and fertility treatments, insomnia, asthma, haemmorrages, heart palpitations and weakness, hearing and earache.

Emotional healing: For creating a balance between being open to love and trust, and not giving or loving too much or over-identifying with your partner or would-be lover.

Chakra: Heart.

Candle colour: *Pink.*

Fragrances: *Almond blossom, apple blossom, cherry blossom, magnolia, rose.*

Practical uses: *Wear pink topaz to take away sadness if you have been hurt in love and have shut yourself away from people to heal your sorrow; a wonderful gift to a first love.*

Magical significance: *Pink topaz brings good luck in love. Write in the air over it, in rose incense-stick smoke or the index finger of the hand you do not write with, the name of the person you desire or "whoever will make me happy and I him/her".*

Divinatory meaning: *If you have been hurt, go slowly in new love so you feel secure at every stage; do not rush from a broken commitment to a new one.*

Zodiac: *Taurus.*

Empowerment: *I am willing to take a risk and trust again.*

Pink topaz, untreated, is found in Pakistan and Russia and is one of the most valuable forms of topaz. The first artificial pink topaz was created in 1750, when a Parisian jeweller discovered that the much more common yellow topaz turns pink if exposed to moderate heat. Pink topaz is very hard and so is one of the more powerful pink crystals, representing realistic love; it eases obsessing over unattainable love or waiting in hope for an indifferent person to soften.

Like all topaz, the pink form helps uncover falsehoods and illusions; if held or worn, it will enable you to distinguish groundless fears (that love will not last or that you are not good or beautiful enough) from real doubts about fidelity or intention.

RED JASPER

Type: Silicate, microcrystalline quartz, here with a high iron content that makes it red.

Colours: Red to terracotta red-brown, sometimes mixed with other minerals to give black line designs.

Availability: Common.

Physical benefits: May help circulation, anaemia, blood cells and blood toxicity, menstruation, safe childbirth and reduction of labour pains, burns, scalds, arthritis, rheumatism, sense of smell, circulation, fertility especially if undergoing treatment for conception; heart conditions, bypass and transplants, exhaustion.

Emotional healing: Gives men and woman quiet strength to resist bullying or domestic violence; offers emotional stability if a serious illness is in remission or during a long treatment where the outcome is uncertain.

Chakra: Root.

Candle colour: *Red.*
Fragrances: *Basil, dragon's blood, garlic, mint.*
Practical uses: *A winter or cold-day crystal; wear red jasper jewellery or keep crystals in your gloves when not wearing them and add red jasper elixir to warm drinks.*
Magical significance: *Protective against psychic attack or if working with spirit rescue, potentially violent or psychologically disturbed people; wear two or three items of red jasper jewellery or a pouch of three small tumblestones round your neck or waist.*
Divinatory meaning: *Be tough but kind with someone close who acts helpless and drains you of money or energy with constant demands.*
Zodiac: *Aries.*
Empowerment: *I am a high achiever.*

According to Viking and German legend, the hilt of the magical sword of Siegfried, the dragon-slayer, was inlaid with red jasper to give him courage. It is therefore a power stone for every man who struggles to make his mark in a competitive and often ruthless world. Called by some Native North Americans the blood of Mother Earth and in Ancient Egypt linked with the fertilizing blood of Mother Isis, the first single-parent deity, red jasper strengthens mothers (and indeed fathers) who bring up children alone. A stone of passion, red jasper is a token of all who consummate love.

BRECCIATED JASPER

Type: Silicate, microcrystalline quartz; red jasper that contains haematite.

Colours: Dark or brick reds, patterned with brown, black and beige swirls and/or clear crystal inclusions.

Availability: Relatively common.

Physical benefits: Believed to help allergies, liver, stomach upsets, digestive disorders, eczema, psoriasis and skin problems aggravated by stress.

Emotional healing: Helps to assimilate and calm emotional responses, sexual problems stemming from self-doubtor guilt.

Chakra: Root, Sacral.

Brecciated jasper has strong grounding energies so is useful during periods of instability or for dealing practically with a crisis. It is an excellent crystal to wear if you are involved with animals, especially when a pet is in need of healing. Keep with precious objects to prevent accidents. Brecciated jasper can be used to cleanse the aura and improve dream recall.

It offers a sense of vitality and strength, increasing self-confidence, creative inspiration. It also helps to enhance physical endurance and performance stamina.

Candle colour: *Red.*
Fragrances: *Benzoin, orange, rosemary.*
Practical uses: *Bury small pieces against a boundary fence if you have nasty neighbours; a tumblestone in a child's room can prevent nightmares.*
Magical significance: *Breaks the psychological/psychic hold of those who seek to manipulate or dominate.*
Divinatory meaning: *An unpleasant colleague should not intimidate you.*
Zodiac: *Virgo and Scorpio.*
Empowerment: *Each dawn brings new inspiration.*

BIXBITE/RED BERYL

Type: Beryl, ring silicate, sometimes called the red emerald.

Colours: Red to pinkish red.

Availability: Rare as gem quality, obtainable in specialist crystal stores and jewellers and online.

Physical benefits: Thought to be good for heart, liver, lungs, mouth, throat, stomach, ulcers of all kinds, chilblains and all winter chills, gradually raising and maintaining physical energy levels; good for anyone who is chronically ill or very old who feels the cold.

Emotional healing: A stone to overcome grief and emotional heartbreak, loss and betrayal, to open the Heart chakra energy centre to future love.

Chakra: Heart.

Candle colour: *Red.*
Fragrances: *Anise, dragon's blood, hibiscus, poppy, thyme.*
Practical uses: *A crystal of warm, affectionate lasting love; wear or carry bixbite to attract someone with whom you are compatible and to keep a relationship caring and supportive even in bad times.*
Magical significance: *Use in love magic to call your twin soul by holding the bixbite up to candlelight at midnight and asking your other half to find you. Blow out the candle and sleep with bixbite taped close to your heart.*
Divinatory meaning: *You may be tempted to act impulsively and unwisely; consider the consequences carefully.*
Zodiac: *Aries and Taurus*
Empowerment: *I value lasting love and loyalty rather than excitement.*

Bixbite is a powerful protector against all who would manipulate or deceive. Wear or tape it close to your navel to meet someone whose charm or persuasion you find hard to resist, whether personal or sales talk.

A stone of passion, bixbite will kindle sexual desire if you love someone but are afraid because of previously bad sexual experiences. A good wedding or pre-wedding gift, it reminds you of the reason for marrying. Also a stone of reconciliation after betrayal, to set between you as you try to find a way back.

Also will help you to heal family estrangements, especially if you quarrelled over a love choice; also helps to create necessary channels if you have to talk to your ex-partner's new love about your children.

RUBY

Type: Corundum (aluminium oxide silicate).

Colours: Pinkish red, purple-red, deep rich to dark ruby red; the most valuable are deep red with a slight blue tinge called pigeon's blood ruby.

Availability: Common to relatively rare, depending on quality and colour.

Physical benefits: May help with infections, circulation, heart, energy, female fertility, male impotence; menstrual problems, early menopause, fibromyalgia, gynaecological operations, pregnancy – particularly for older women.

Emotional healing: Helps the sharing of loving energy despite past hurt; reduces fear of the paranormal and evil.

Chakra: Heart.

Candle colour: *Red.*
Fragrances: *Allspice, basil, carnation, cinnamon, dragon's blood, red rose.*
Practical uses: *Protects the home from fire and intruders; wear discreetly to stay safe at night.*
Magical significance: *Guards against psychic and psychological attack (it is said to darken in the presence of a liar); wear during lovemaking to conceive and maintain/restore passion.*
Divinatory meaning: *Value friends and family even if they seem temporarily dull.*
Zodiac: *Cancer and Sagittarius.*
Empowerment: *My fears have no reality and I let them go.*

The ruby is one of the four precious gemstones (the others are diamond, emerald and sapphire) worn since ancient times to signify high status.

It is most commonly associated with love, especially faithful passionate commitment, and helps older women to value their beauty and life experience. Rubies bring prophetic dreams and banish nightmares; to dream of rubies is a sign of coming prosperity and good fortune.

Tumblestones at home for each family member will maintain loving links wherever they are.

Red Carnelian

Type: Chalcedony.

Colours: Red-brown, red, reddish orange, the active male energy stone, distinguished by its glowing vibrant colour.

Availability: Common, especially as tumblestone.

Physical benefits: May help with exhaustion, lack of energy, ME, male potency and sex drive; male genital disorders; improve appetite; cleanse the blood; for circulation, the gall bladder, liver, spleen, jaundice, digestive disorders; stimulate self-healing of the body; rheumatism, bone, joint pains and arthritis especially in men.

Emotional healing: Alleviates jealousy and possessiveness in relationships; helps anger management; a dish of vibrant carnelians in the home absorbs fury from toddlers, teenagers and adults of both sexes; assists with the male mid-life crisis: wash crystals weekly.

Chakra: Solar Plexus.

A stone of the sun, male-energy carnelian is ideal for women who need to assert themselves or make a major personal leap. Roman carnelian rings or seals engraved with deity images or fierce animals were considered both protective and lucky.

Red carnelian is seen as a stone of passion: place it beneath the four corners of the mattress or circled round a red candle in the bedroom before lovemaking. It is also useful for giving confidence for performances on stage or live media work, and guards the home from theft, fire, storm, loss or accident.

Candle colour: *Bright orange.*

Fragrances: *Cedar, ginger, juniper, pine, sagebrush.*

Practical uses: *Protects against poverty and attracts prosperity; wear carnelian when funds are low to draw resources and good luck into your life; good for success in any creative money-spinning ventures.*

Magical significance: *If you have a powerful urgent desire or need courage, light a circle of eight red candles; pass carnelian jewellery or a lucky vibrant carnelian three times over them. Then light a carnelian-fragrance incense stick and draw a lion or a bear over the carnelian in incense smoke to empower it.*

Divinatory meaning: *Not a time to back down; ask for what you need and do not settle for second best.*

Zodiac: *Leo.*

Empowerment: *I will not underestimate myself.*

RED CALCITE

Type: Calcium carbonate.

Colours: Usually pale red, but can be reddish pink to orangish red with clear streaks.

Availability: Common.

Physical benefits: Thought to assist with all menstrual problems, especially irregular ovulation, ovarian cysts, endometriosis, amenorrhea, painful menstruation; help to improve circulation and cleanse the blood; can help kidneys and pancreas.

Emotional healing: For anyone expressing anger in inappropriate ways, by self-harming or seeking unnecessary medical attention or frequent panic attacks; for people who are hooked on psychic or sex phone lines or who seek love through indiscriminate sex; over-control as in obsessive compulsive disorder.

Chakra: Sacral and Root.

Associated with the veins of Mother Earth that carry her life blood to her children; in the north of Scandinavia some people still ask permission of the rock before cutting it. Red calcite helps us to understand our karmic patterns and so to avoid repeating the same mistakes or being constantly attracted to the wrong kind of person.

Keep red calcite with you when you consummate a relationship for the first time, particularly after a long period of celibacy or if you are very anxious.

Candle colour: *Pale red.*
Fragrances: *Acacia, almond, hibiscus, poppy, rose.*
Practical uses: *Gives children and teenagers courage to stand up to bullies without becoming aggressive themselves; also for timid animals who are bullied by others in the home or streets.*
Magical significance: *To rekindle passion in a long-standing relationship, light rose-scented candles in the bathroom; add a smooth natural red calcite to your bath along with your favourite rose essence; gently massage your body with it, chanting softly, "I call my love with fire and with fragrance, with fragrance and with fire".*
Divinatory meaning: *You have every right to be angry with someone close. Consider their good qualities before responding.*
Zodiac: *Scorpio.*
Empowerment: *I will not only survive but thrive.*

ZINCITE

Type: Zinc oxide, the ore of zinc (see also schalenblende).

Colours: Red, red-orange, orange-yellow to deep brown.

Availability: Obtainable from specialist crystal stores and online.

Physical benefits: Thought to assist wound healing, prostate gland, female and male genitalia and reproductive organs, libido, fertility, HIV, AIDS, auto-immune diseases, bronchitis, resistance to colds and influenza.

Emotional healing: Overcomes crippling worries about failure and getting hurt that prevent participation in employment or relationships; good if you have been burned by previous bad experiences.

Chakra: Root, Sacral, Solar Plexus.

Candle colour: *Orange.*

Fragrances: *Carnation, ginger, hibiscus, orange, sage.*

Practical uses: *Associated with property, home buying and selling; carry zincite when house hunting to identify the right home for you; keep on display when prospective buyers visit your home.*

Magical significance: *Associated with dragons and dragon energies in magic, empower zincite for good fortune, prosperity or fertility using either candle or fire magic.*

Divinatory meaning: *You will meet a useful like-minded person to help get a venture off the ground.*

Zodiac: *Taurus and Libra.*

Empowerment: *I call creative energies into my life.*

Called by indigenous peoples the life blood of the Earth Mother, zincite is abundant in New Jersey, USA, but quite rare elsewhere. It has also grown as a result of a fire at an old Polish zinc-smelting works, hence falls between man-made and natural.

Zincite activates the lower chakras of the body that in turn energize the higher ones. A small piece brings a tremendous feeling of wellbeing, energy and vitality. Even those not particularly sensitive to crystal energies will be able to experience and benefit from its charge.

Zincite enhances all creative energies. It should be used with caution as it is so powerful and is not suitable for children or animals.

COPPER NUGGET

Type: Metal nuggets.

Colours: Burnished golden-reddish bronze.

Availability: Common.

Physical benefits: May help balance energies, clear blockages, rheumatism, arthritis, stiffness and swellings of hands and feet; helpfu with infected wounds, fertility, weight loss; and worn over the navel for travel sickness.

Emotional healing: Helps connections grow with other people if you find it hard to socialize or are necessarily apart from friends and family.

Chakra: Heart.

Copper brings good luck to the home: nuggets traditionally insulate against storm, fire and flood and attract good visitors. It opens energy pathways and attracts the right people and resources into your life. Carry when travelling to find the right facilities and to minimize delays. Hold on your Heart chakra to balance your entire energy system, remove any blockages or negativity and draw up earth energy outdoors. A crystal nugget will amplify the powers of other crystals if placed within a circle of copper nuggets for a few hours.

Candle colour: *Green.*

Fragrances: *Lilac, lily, mimosa, rose, violet.*

Practical uses: *A copper ring on your wedding finger brings love; on the opposite hand it attracts new friends.*

Magical significance: *To attract money to your life, place a nugget in a ceramic pot with a lid; add a copper coin every day until full, then give the money to charity.*

Divinatory meaning: *Start a dialogue with someone you would like to know better, as the other person would welcome contact.*

Zodiac: *Taurus.*

Empowerment: *Life flows in and around me harmoniously.*

FIRE OPAL

Type: Hydrated silicon dioxide. Fire opal is a type of opal (the others are common and precious) and is called precious fire opal if it displays iridescent flashes of colours within it when it is moved.

Colours: Bright orange to red, glowing.

Physical benefits: May help abdomen, lower back, kidneys, genitals, intestines, adrenal glands, libido, orgasm, fertility, iron deficiency and blood disorders.

Emotional healing: Awakens personal power to cope courageously with emotional turmoil or unwelcome change; heals sexual and domestic abuse andtrauma.

Chakra: Solar Plexus.

In Mexico, fire opal was called by the Aztecs the stone of the bird of paradise after their feathered serpent creator god, Quetzalcoatl. This power to stimulate creativity and new beginnings, as well as necessary destruction, makes fire opal the most active of the opals. It can be worn as a charm by anyone who wants to be independent and live by their own rules, or to make their mark professionally or personally. It is also a stone that gives courage to find passionate, lasting love with someone of whom your family or friends would disapprove.

Candle colour: *Red.*

Fragrances: *Allspice, anise, benzoin, copal, ginger.*

Practical uses: *Good for tackling major issues and facing up to people.*

Magical significance: *A focus for candle magic, both to attract money and to bring passion into a relationship. Name the purpose as you pass the opal round a red candle flame nine times (not too close, as heat can damage it).*

Divinatory meaning: *Straight talking and decisive actions are necessary.*

Zodiac: *Aries.*

Empowerment: *I can tackle problems head-on.*

ORANGE CARNELIAN

Type: Chalcedony.

Colours: Orange-pinkish and softer paler orange, the receptive or passive female energy stone, also occasionally yellowish orange, pink or almost brown.

Availability: Common, especially as tumblestones.

Physical benefits: Believed to aid female fertility, IVF and artificial insemination, PMS, menstrual and menopausal symptoms, kidneys, colds, cuts, wounds, blood disorders, heart palpitations, hay fever, recovery after illness, surgery, accident or trauma.

Emotional healing: Overcomes sexual anxieties, vaginismus, failure to reach orgasm; eating disorders.

Chakra: Sacral.

Candle colour: *Orange.*
Fragrances: *Chamomile, hibiscus, marigold, orange, rosemary.*
Practical uses: *Pink-hued carnelian adjusts a couple to parenthood.*
Magical significance: *Set two carnelians in front of an orange candle, call your twin soul, blow out the candle then cast the crystals into running water or a deep lake.*
Divinatory meaning: *You may get the chance to breathe new life into a relationship.*
Zodiac: *Virgo and Sagittarius.*
Empowerment: *I am as courageous as a lioness.*

The Ancient Egyptians called carnelian the setting sun. They associated it with the fertile menstrual blood of the mother goddess Isis.

The hieroglyph tjet (below), representing the girdle of Isis, was drawn or engraved on carnelian or red jasper by women seeking help from Isis. You can draw the tjet in incense-stick smoke over a carnelian if you need help with improving fertility.

WULFENITE

Type: Sulphates, lead molybdate.

Colours: Orange, red and yellow.

Availability: Common, but with a varying price range as some specimens are highly collectible.

Physical benefits: Seen as being helpful with menopause and menstrual cycles, female reproductive problems, including endometriosis and uterine fibroids, restores appetite and aids digestion and the spleen.

Emotional healing: Balances emotions and invigorates passion to heal failing relationships; enables us to acknowledge our own shadow negative side and that of others without becoming resentful or guilty.

Chakra: Solar Plexus, Sacral and Root.

Candle colour: *Orange.*
Fragrances: *Bay, lemon, galbanum, geranium, hibiscus, peppermint.*
Practical uses: *Encourages environmental awareness.*
Magical significance: *Aids psychic development, especially through tuning into nature's forces.*
Divinatory meaning: *A chance to express a creative gift in a way that will get tangible positive rewards, but also involves effort and the risk of standing out from the crowd.*
Zodiac: *Sagittarius.*
Empowerment: *I accept that sometimes I have negative feelings.*

First described by Austrian mineralogist Franz Xavier Von Wulfen in 1785, and named after him, wulfenite is the crystal of the Solar Plexus chakra energy centre, associated with the physical sun and our inner sun.

It is a crystal of clearing emotional blockages and expressing our true selves so that our inner and outer selves harmonize. This crystal enables us to reach out in our relationships with balanced giving and taking.

WARNING: Do not use to make elixirs, gem water or massage oil as it contains poisonous lead and molybdate.

LIMONITE

Type: Hydrated iron oxide, composed mainly of goethite.

Colours: Yellow, yellow-brown, red-brown.

Availability: Common.

Physical benefits: Said to promote the healing of blood, lungs and liver disorders; used in Chinese medicine for intestines, stomach and general digestive disorders; is believed to relieve IBS and chronic diarrhoea.

Emotional healing: Calming and grounding in the fast 24/7 world; for those alone in life, gives a sense of kinship with others, encourages home-making and may guide a mate or like-minded companion to you.

Chakra: Root or Sacral.

Candle colour: *Yellow.*
Fragrances: *Benzoin, cloves, geranium, myrrh, rosemary.*
Practical uses: *Protects against psychic, psychological and physical negativity. Used as artists' pigment (ochre) and for ancient cave art and so represents in Australian Aboriginal culture, beauty and creativity given by Mother Earth.*
Magical significance: *Helps to focus psychic abilities and improves visionary skills; used in earth healing rituals and for rites of passage as red (limonite oxide) and yellow; any piece of limonite carries ancient genetic memory that enables you to tap into earth power.*
Divinatory meaning: *Do not let a negative reaction of someone deter you from a slower lifestyle.*
Zodiac: *Virgo.*
Empowerment: *I welcome the fertility of the earth.*

Every newly built or impersonal modern home, soulless hotel room or workplace benefits from a piece of limonite to make it feel more welcoming; if you have an intrusive landlord or lady, flatmates or neighbours, this crystal creates stability and marks your own territory.

Keep also in the car to hold if your satellite navigation is giving you false information, to guide you home or to a chosen destination. Hold it over the place you need to be on the map and say, "Take me there." Place also near the tank or cage of an exotic pet to help them feel safe; good for researching family history and locating distant family members.

LEMON CHRYSOPRASE

Type: Chalcedony gem variety with nickel; alternatively light yellow magnesite with brown to light tan veining.

Colours: Lemon yellow to yellow-green.

Availability: Common.

Physical benefits: May assist with skin, muscles, mobility, nausea especially in pregnancy, diarrhoea, weight loss, liver, cholesterol, detoxification, hormone imbalance, sexual dysfunction, headaches (food-related), saliva and sweat glands, recovery after illness or surgery.

Emotional healing: Good for breaking free of emotional blackmail, manipulation and mind games.

Chakra: Heart and Solar Plexus.

Wear or carry and touch lemon chrysoprase to deter undesirable people from bothering you at night when travelling home. Give a tumblestone or as jewellery to any family member who is jealous of an addition, or if your new partner resents your children; also makes established pets accept new animals. The crystal benefits from occasional rehydration with water. Will reduce the pains of unrequited love; carry to deter a would-be lover who refuses to take no for an answer.

Encourages honesty; touch one to sense the intention to deceive as you will feel an icy tingling in your fingers.

Candle colour: *Lemon yellow.*
Fragrances: *Bergamot, grapefruit, lemon.*
Practical uses: *Bury by the front door to deter unwanted callers; wear to protect against emotional pressure.*
Magical significance: *Empower to break hexes or attempts to control your mind by naming the perpetrator as you hold the stone; seal in a plastic container in the freezer; bury both after three months.*
Divinatory meaning: *You may hear something shocking; do not take it seriously as the teller has a hidden agenda.*
Zodiac: *Gemini.*
Empowerment: *All will be resolved in its own time.*

CHRYSOBERYL

Type: Aluminium oxide containing beryllium, the official cat's eye in lustrous eye form.

Colours: Clear yellow, honey, yellowy green or brown.

Availability: Relatively rare.

Physical benefits: Claimed to relieve disorders connected with exhaustion; diarrhoea, IBS, coeliac disease, stomach ulcers and other intestinal disorders, food allergies and intolerances; chest infections; improves resistance to illness; good for eyesight, particularly night vision and clear-sightedness; encourages gentle weight loss by natural means.

Emotional healing: Good for people who adopt the opinions and values of whomever they are with, to see life through their own eyes and develop a personal identity.

Chakra: Solar Plexus.

Most special of the chrysoberyls is the lustrous cat's eye, also known as cymophane. This is not faceted but carved into cabochons, highly polished domed shapes. It is a luck-bringer and protective against mishaps. The two other gem varieties of chrysoberyl are the faceted, transparent yellowish-green to green, yellow and brown version and emerald-green alexandrite.

Chrysoberyl enhances healing properties of other crystals or alternative remedies. All chrysoberyls are prosperity-bringers and were once believed to attract a wealthy partner. They represent the ability to strive for the best and highest standards in ethics, success and achievement.

Candle colour: *Yellow or gold.*

Fragrances: *Marigold, mimosa, mint, rosemary, thyme.*

Practical uses: *Associated traditionally with great leaders, a good gem to wear if you have organize a sports, community, charity or social event such as a wedding or christening if you know there will be interference.*

Magical significance: *Wear or hold to increase telepathic communication with your cat or other intelligent pets such as dogs or horses, particularly if you are late home and want to reassure them.*

Divinatory meaning: *Look for long-term advantage and security if contemplating change, and consider if you might be better be off where you are.*

Zodiac: *Gemini or Leo.*

Empowerment: *I do not need to follow the lead of others.*

GOLDEN/ YELLOW CALCITE

Type: Calcium carbonate.

Colours: From pale yellow through shades of yellow to gold.

Availability: Common.

Physical benefits: Seen as aiding the detoxification of all digestive organs.

Emotional healing: Self-esteem that has been damaged by abuse, coldness or neglect in childhood or later in life by a destructive or controlling relationship; assists body-image issues.

Chakra: Solar Plexus and Sacral.

Use for healing pets or for soothing rescued or lost animals; add the natural crystal to the pet's water for a few hours; also helps pets who are jealous of a new family member to minimize aggression. Set tumbled stone in healing or home empowerment/protection layouts to spread the energy through the grid and into the patient or the home.

The more golden the stone, the more powerful its properties; a golden calcite sphere expands the boundaries of what is possible through our own efforts rather than luck. An excellent crystal if you are a mature student or want to retrain.

Candle colour: *Gold.*

Fragrances: *Anise, copal, frankincense, sandalwood, sage.*

Practical uses: *Melts resentment and estrangement and, if worn, attracts friendships and social opportunities.*

Magical significance: *Write down the names of anyone spiteful, fold the list as small as possible and tie it with three knots with a piece of yellow calcite in a yellow scarf. Keep in a drawer.*

Divinatory meaning: *A routine social event will be better than expected. Accept the invitation.*

Zodiac: *Sagittarius and Pisces*

Empowerment: *I will make today golden.*

KEYIAPO STONE

Type: Iron pyrites/marcasite with quartz.

Colours: Golden.

Availability: Rare but worth searching out.

Physical benefits: Thought to be beneficial for male genito-urinary system, impotence, low sperm count, hernia, prostate, energizer for men and women, scanty or irregular menstruation; it is believed that this is a stone that, if held in the hand you write with for men and the opposite for women, rebalances the whole system, removing impurities and toxins if you move it slowly up the body, feet to crown, a few centimetres away.

Emotional healing: Brings a sense of certainty of your own worth if you have always been told you are wrong or stupid; fills the whole self with a sense of abundance and self-containment if you worry about being left alone and so stay in an unsatisfactory relationship.

Chakra: Root and Solar Plexus.

Keyiapo stones have returned to the marketplace after they appeared and reappeared during the early 1990s, but are still quite elusive. They are a very powerful healing stone if no other remedy seems to be working, and on a daily level they bring energy and a sense of well-being.

Women who wish to conceive an infant should hold the golden stone for a few minutes every night before lovemaking.

Candle colour: *Gold.*

Fragrances: *Copal, dragon's blood, frankincense, galbanum.*

Practical uses: *Keyiapo protects against free-floating anxieties. Hold your stone if you start fretting; allow the golden energies to transform fear into positive thought.*

Magical significance: *Hold your keyiapo stone in open cupped hands so gold candlelight shines on it; focus on it until your eyes are tired, then close them; picture the golden Akashic records, books said to contain all knowledge of past, present and future; ask a question and you will see the answer.*

Divinatory meaning: *A golden opportunity seems just out of reach; if you go all-out to reach it there is a good chance, though not certainty, you will succeed.*

Zodiac: *Aries.*

Empowerment: *I have more than enough for my needs.*

Turritella Agate

Type: Agate with a thick coating of fossilised sea shells.

Colours: Brown or black with coloured inclusions, mainly brown, black, white circular patterns.

Availability: Common.

Physical benefits: May relieve exhaustion, swellings of hands or feet, skin rashes and lesions, varicose veins, sexual dysfunction; alleviates problems of ageing, digestion, gastro-enteritis and gallstone pain; assist with the absorption of minerals.

Emotional healing: Helps overcome past grievances standing in the way of harmonious relationships: if healing others, turritella in a pocket or pouch unlocks deep-seated trauma being manifest as physical symptoms and phobias.

Chakra: Root.

Brings connections with your personal past: your ancestors, homeland and the country from which your ancestors came. Heals the earth if buried in land that has been neglected or polluted or placed on a map or photo of an endangered area. An excellent fertility crystal, also helpful for increasing chances of success with IVF, artificial insemination and other fertility treatments. Give to a person who always plays the victim. A stone for meditation, as gazing into one induces a trance state; also for allowing therapeutic hypnotism to work better if you find it hard to relax.

Candle colour: *Brown.*
Fragrances: *Lavender, rose, sagebrush.*
Practical uses: *A survival stone. Keep one in the centre of your home to unite the family or to give yourself roots.*
Workplace: *If you travel a lot for work, it will protect you from danger, alleviate fears and keeps you connected with loved ones at home.*
Magical significance: *Acts as record keeper crystal, so gives access to the wisdom of past worlds and past life recall or dreams.*
Divinatory meaning: *Value what you are and where you have come from.*
Zodiac: *Capricorn*
Empowerment: *I acknowledge my roots and so I can grow strong in my own pattern.*

SCHALENBLENDE

Type: Zinc iron sulphide.

Colours: Brown, yellow-brown, beige, silver-grey, blue, banded, undulating appearance.

Availability: Found in specialist crystal stores and online.

Physical benefits: Thought to assist with recovery of physical wounds, diabetes, immune system, cell regeneration, sense of smell, taste and vision, prostate gland, genitalia, preconception health and fertility.

Emotional healing: Helps recognize and safely release pent-up anxieties; for getting over a bad relationship.

Chakra: Root.

Schalenblende is an attractive stone of compacted layers of several minerals, usually sphalerite and wurtzite (both varieties of zinc iron sulphide), galena and/or pyrite. Traditionally it is a stone of protection during travel to spiritual realms. Helpful for all property matters and for changing bad luck into good. A powerful crystal for bringing together different people to create a team, whether to fix your home, get a project off the ground, form a social or healing group or for organizing a small party so everyone will mix; good for wedding planners and all who arrange events.

Candle colour: *Cream or brown.*
Fragrances: *Dragon's blood, galbanum, lemon verbena, mugwort, patchouli.*
Practical uses: *Obtain a polished piece to guide you to what you need when you need it.*
Magical significance: *A fertility charm; also banishes undesirable influences from your life; bury a piece where nothing grows late at night on the waning moon.*
Divinatory meaning: *An ongoing disagreement between yourself and a loved one will be resolved.*
Zodiac: *Capricorn and Aquarius*
Empowerment: *I replace negative with positive energies.*

FRANKLINITE

Type: Oxide/zinc manganese iron oxide/spinel family.

Colours: Black, brown-black, metallic.

Availability: Relatively rare.

Physical benefits: Thought to assist with hair growth, vision, male reproductive system, resistance to colds and influenza, discovering new treatments and cures for stubborn illnesses.

Emotional healing: Brings sudden insight to emotional problems; teaches difference between truth and illusion and what should be preserved and what let go where these areas are blurred due to immaturity or psychological blockages.

Chakra: Root.

Mined at Franklin, New Jersey, franklinite has strong grounding energies that build up over time as practical results for all forms of healing work or spiritual development. Can trigger the subconscious to reveal hidden messages and act as a wakeup call for future problems. A mineral of diplomacy, franklinite is a welcome addition to a home or workplace where banter tips over into sarcasm; also helpful for detering an over-enthusiastic would-be lover. A survival crystal for hard financial times when money-making combines single-mindedness in economizing with ingenuity.

Candle colour: *Dark purple or dark brown.*
Fragrances: *Allspice, cinnamon, ginger, hibiscus, juniper.*
Practical uses: *A talisman for rebuilding relationships; avoids wallowing in the past, but confronts issues that caused the problems.*
Magical significance: *The weak magnetic charge makes this good for drawing what you want into your life; programme the crystal by holding it and stating what you need and picturing the outcome.*
Divinatory meaning: *Be inventive and create opportunites.*
Zodiac: *Gemini*
Empowerment: *I can reinvent myself.*

SMOKY QUARTZ

Type: Quartz (also called cairngorm).

Colours: Tinted smoky brown or dark grey by natural radiation.

Availability: Common.

Physical benefits: After a period of illness or depression this is said to be good for gently restoring physical energy, melting energy blocks or rigidity in limbs, the adrenal glands, kidneys (good for kidney stones) and the pancreas; also believed to help with the relief of chronic pain.

Emotional healing: Reduces anxiety, psychological sexual blocks, insomnia, self-harming and panic attacks.

Chakra: Root (opens the chakra gently).

A guardian against bad luck; in Switzerland, Germany and Austria, smoky quartz crucifixes were traditionally put on bedroom walls to keep away evil, especially at night.

Use smoky quartz to absorb misfortune, sorrows or seemingly impossible obstacles by standing with a pointed smoky quartz in each hand, point downwards towards the earth. Imagine whatever you need to shed pouring through your fingertips and the crystals into Mother Earth. If you can do this outdoors, afterwards plant some seeds or flowers, or indoors put a small herb into a pot.

Candle colour: *Indigo.*
Fragrances: *Cedar, cypress, hibiscus, lily, mimosa, patchouli.*
Practical uses: *Protects the home, vehicles and possessions against theft, damage and accidents caused by human error; keep one in a purse or bag in the glove box of a car or near valuables, especially if they are unattended for long periods.*
Magical significance: *Smoky quartz is said to create an astral pathway to past worlds or out-of-body travel if you shine candlelight into its centre and follow the pathway in your mind; protects against nasty spirits.*
Divinatory meaning: *There is light at the end of the tunnel; you will slowly see improvements in a long-standing worry soon.*
Zodiac: *Capricorn.*
Empowerment: *I walk in hope towards the future, even if it seems uncertain right now.*

DINOSAUR BONE

Type: Agatized dinosaur bone is fossilized bone from dinosaurs in which the cellular structure has been replaced with quartz, leaving the bone structure intact.

Colours: Brown, grey, white or black for natural; agatized as brown to black with splashes of red, blue and bright yellow; occasionally yellow-gold and red.

Availability: Becoming rarer as collection is restricted. Physical benefits: Said to be good for bone strength and fracture healing, bone marrow, DNA and all hereditary conditions, relief of chronic pain, lifelong illnesses.

Emotional healing: Soothes grief after the death of a long-term mate, a child or the breakdown of a relationship.

Chakra: Root.

Even the smallest piece of fossilized bone carries millions of years of the world's history within it; totally natural relics are even more magical than their more polished cousins. Hold when you are tired or others are taking your power away; draw strength from accumulated ancient Earth power, one of the most powerful and yet soothing energizers; bury a small natural dinosaur bone near the doorstep of a newly built house or in any wall, fireplace, new conservatory, extension or conversion. This will bring good fortune to the home and protect against teething problems.

Candle colour: *Grey.*
Fragrances: *Cypress, lavender, musk, sage*
Practical uses: *Good if you have older relatives living with you to help them feel part of the family.*
Magical significance: *Connects the wearer with the wisdom of many ages, bringing spontaneous recall of past lives and worlds.*
Divinatory meaning: *Do not make the same mistake you have done before when dealing with a manipulative person; stand strong.*
Zodiac: *Capricorn*
Empowerment: *The past holds the key to the future.*

Apophyllite

Type: Sheet silicate, phylosillicate group.

Colours: Usually colourless/white, can contain rainbows or shine like mother-of-pearl where surface is fractured; also pale green, but can take on other colours such as pale pink from the presence of other minerals.

Availability: Obtainable from specialist crystal stores and online.

Physical benefits: Thought to help to ease asthma, cystic fibrosis, hay fever, emphysema and other respiratory problems; skin including eczema; called the Reiki crystal because its effects are said to be similar to a Reiki treatment (heal with an apophyllite point); may regularize heartbeat and pulse.

Emotional healing: Place a point or pointed apophyllite on your third eye/brow energy centre to make you feel whole and retrieve what you unwisely but in love have given away of your identity to others; green is best for emotional healing and spiritual work.

Chakra: Heart and Brow.

Apophyllite draws negativity from other crystals used in healing or around the home. A crystal that as a cluster brings people together emotionally; for healing fractured love or family relationships, especially when outsiders are interfering or there are divided loyalties within or caused by step-family relationships; for action in fulfilling major desired house moves or additions to the family; encourages saving and wise use of financial resources.

Candle colour: *White.*

Fragrances: *Chamomile, lemon, lime, tea tree, violet.*

Practical uses: *Keep an apophyllite cluster near the centre of the room where you relax as it will automatically cleanse the whole space, Feng Shui style. Pass incense smoke over the crystal monthly to keep it clear.*

Magical significance: *A crystal of connection with beings of other dimensions from power animals to spirit guides. Hold colourless apophyllite in sun, moon or candlelight to discover your personal guides and angels or increase communication.*

Divinatory meaning: *Check and recheck plans and make sure you are up to date with paperwork and official forms.*

Zodiac: *Gemini, Aquarius.*

Empowerment: *I can take action rather than waiting for the cosmos to deliver.*

WINDOW QUARTZ

Type: Quartz, usually clear, with a diamond window as an extra seventh face.

Colours: Most usually in clear quartz .

Availability: Relatively rare.

Physical benefits: May help with eyesight, finding new treatments for existing conditions via the Internet; send concentrated healing energy by holding the window on a painful spot.

Emotional healing: A crystal for accepting imperfections in self and others; helpful for anyone suddenly disabled through an accident, injury or illness, to cope psychologically.

Chakra: Brow.

Window quartz, particularly in its clear, sparkling quartz form, is a master crystal, assisting with natural acquisition of spiritual wisdom for beginner and expert alike. Hold the diamond to the centre of your brow to connect with angels, guides and your wise family ancestors.

Window quartz is helpful if you are trying to gain insight into the motives of others, for example why someone has an apparently irrational dislike of you, why a lover will not commit, and also into your own seemingly self-destructive actions.

Candle colour: *White.*
Fragrances: *Juniper, pine.*
Practical uses: *Keep by your computer for safe communication with people abroad.*
Magical significance: *Use to locate missing people by remote viewing; look through the window in sunlight or moonlight and you will see an image of what you are seeking and the background may give you a clue.*
Divinatory meaning: *Good news will clear up something that has been worrying you.*
Zodiac: *Leo.*
Empowerment: *The future is clear.*

RAINBOW MOONSTONE

Type: Feldspar.

Colours: Milky white with rainbow sheen/flashes.
Availability: Rarer than ordinary moonstone, but relatively
easily obtainable.

Physical benefits: Thought to assist with hormones,
fertility, menstrual cycle, thyroid, pituitary gland, bowels,
breasts, recovery after operations on breasts, womb,
sterilization, anaphylactic shock.

Emotional healing: Combining gentle lunar energies with
the optimism of the rainbow, reassures all who feel alone,
lost or vulnerable; assists all emotional healing.

Chakra: Sacral, Brow, Crown.

This white labradorite variety of feldspar offers an
intensified colour-spectrum sensation. Place under
your pillow or where it catches the moon's rays to aid
lucid dreaming and calm sleep, and find your dream
lover. Rainbow moonstone is gentle and will offer
ongoing strength against illness. A supportive stone for
those who consider harming themselves. It may also
improve learning difficulties in young children, and
protects homes in remote areas.

Candle colour: *White or silver.*
Fragrances: *Eucalyptus, jasmine, lemon balm, myrrh, neroli.*
Practical uses: *Plant in the garden three days before full
moon or when you see a rainbow for healthy growth in plants
and attracting butterflies. Also helpful if you are having a
relationship at work.*
Magical significance: *The original mood stone, becomes
brighter or duller in response to mood and energy levels; use in
moon magic.*
Divinatory meaning: *Nurture yourself and take time to
relax.*
Zodiac: *Cancer.*
Empowerment: *I will collect moments of happiness.*

BANDED ONYX

Type: Quartz, chalcedony, a variety of agate, the white banded kind tends not to be heat-treated.

Colours: White with streaks of black, grey or cream; also varieties of orange, brown or green; white banded onyx is often found as broad bands with black onyx.

Availability: Common.

Physical benefits: Thought to help cells, particularly white blood cells, bone marrow, Hodgkinson's disease, lymph glands, thrush, vaginal infections, breasts, teeth, jaw, bone disorders, pregnancy, after a gynaecological or breast operation.

Emotional healing: Restores faith in people.

Chakra: Heart and Crown.

Banded onyx has long been used for ornamental purposes, especially cameos. Now there is a huge array of banded onyx, some dyed or heat-enhanced, some natural, but all equally powerful in its protective energies. White banded bowls enhance and cleanse crystals kept in them, while white or pale banded candle holders increase the luck-attracting and protective powers of the lighted flame. Drink your crystal elixirs from a white onyx cup to increase their potency.

Candle colour: *White.*
Fragrances: *Apple blossom, lily, lily of the valley, lotus, mimosa.*
Practical uses: *For mending lovers' quarrels; exchange matching small white banded onyx ornaments on your wedding or betrothal day.*
Magical significance: *Use a white onyx mortar and pestle for mixing herbs to empower them; before use, put your hands round it and ask that it be filled with light.*
Divinatory meaning: *Check with someone reliable what you have heard about your future.*
Zodiac: *Libra.*
Empowerment: *I seek highest motives in my words and actions.*

CLEAR FLUORITE

Type: Halide, calcium fluoride. Pure fluorite is colourless but trace impurities result in various colours.

Colours: Clear or colourless.

Availability: Relatively common.

Physical benefits: May improve the immune system, eyesight, bones, sinuses, spleen, skin, arthritis, teeth, fight debilitating viruses, colds or infections; assist infant and mother to recover from the shock of medical intervention during birth.

Emotional healing: Helps to bring order out of chaotic personal emotional turmoil or pressure from others and restores clear and positive thinking.

Chakra: Brow.

Clear fluorite cleanses impurities in the body and blockages in mind and spirit. Fluorite angels, spheres and eggs are gentle energizers and break down divisions between our world and angelic realms.

Meditation with this crystal can stimulate latent psychic abilities and enhance intuition that increases level and length of visionary experience. Clear fluorite brings balance during spiritual or psychic development work, and offers protection against malicious spirits and negative energies.

Candle colour: *White or silver.*
Fragrances: *Chamomile, elder, myrrh.*
Practical uses: *Gives gentle energy to sick or recovering children and animals; keep a dish in the kitchen and dining area to encourage a balanced attitude to food.*
Magical significance: *Acts as a pain absorber if you physically place the crystal on affected area; enhances the energies of other crystals so can be used in crystal healing combinations and layouts.*
Divinatory meaning: *You are being offered the best possible deal that will get life moving.*
Zodiac: *Pisces*
Empowerment: *Gentle strength can move mountains.*

CLEAR DANBURITE

Type: Calcium borosilicate produces crystals similar to topaz.

Colours: Colourless, white, sparkling when polished.

Availability: Relatively common; almost all danburite is colourless.

Physical benefits: Gentler than crystal quartz but thought to be equally clear for healing, danburite is believed to help to clear energy blockages throughout the whole body for sick children, old people, smaller animals or anyone who is weak or vulnerable if the sickness is acute; may also ease problems connected with liver, gall bladder, all organs or tissues or inoperable conditions.

Emotional healing: Injects positive feelings into ongoing negative situations and people we cannot walk away from, bringing the best possible outcome; helps us to see good in everyone, however difficult.

Chakra: Heart, Crown.

Clear danburite is a relatively recent discovery, named after Danbury, Connecticut, where it was found in 1839. If you find clear crystal quartz too intense, clear danburite has all its energizing, clearing and light-bringing properties, but is much more an empathic people-orientated crystal, encouraging interconnections between individuals and groups.

It draws people who are in tune with you, so wear or carry one to social events when looking for a partner or communicating via online socializing sites – it deters time-wasters, fantasists and less benign contacts.

Candle colour: *White.*
Fragrances: *Lily, lily of the valley, lotus, musk, white rose.*
Practical uses: *Called the celebration stone because it brings joy to any gathering or party (give a small tumblestone to everyone present as a gift), danburite jewellery is as perfect as the more expensive white sapphire or diamond for betrothals or any celebration to say "I offer you my love".*
Magical significance: *An angel crystal, especially as a clear cluster that in natural or candle light creates a powerful light energy to open visions of your guardian angel.*
Divinatory meaning: *You will see the good side of an uncommunicative older relative and find a lot in common.*
Zodiac: *Aquarius and Leo.*
Empowerment: *I regard everyone as friends unless proved otherwise.*

Twin/Gemini Quartz

Type: Two very similar clear quartz crystals, usually growing from the same base .

Colours: Most common in clear quartz.

Availability: Found in specialist crystal stores and online.

Physical benefits: May help twin and multiple pregnancies, births and after-birth care; back, spine, rib cage.

Emotional healing: Consoling if you cannot be with your true love because of other commitments, to build a good life without totally giving up hope of being together one day.

Chakra: Crown and Brow.

Tantric twin crystals are crystals approximately the same size growing from a common base. Twin souls or soulmates do not grow from the same base but are equal length and size, growing side-by-side. They may join on one side during formation and end in separate terminations. They bring peace to couples, families, workplaces and communities. All twin crystals encourage more openness if twins make another sibling feel left out in a family.

Candle colour: *White.*
Fragrances: *Almond, anise, bay, lavender, lemon verbena.*
Practical uses: *Twin crystals are a good-luck charm for all partnerships.*
Magical significance: *For calling your twin soul in sleep or in rituals, light matching candles, one either side of the twin crystal and place your hands round each twin crystal, asking that you will find your twin soul. Leave the candles to burn.*
Divinatory meaning: *You will encounter someone like-minded who will improve the quality of your life.*
Zodiac: *Gemini.*
Empowerment: *My twin soul is waiting for me.*

BRYOZOAN

Type: Micro-fossils within stones; fossilized portion of an animal colony.

Colours: Blue-grey, grey, brown, black with various markings.

Availability: Relatively rare as tumblestones or jewellery but these are best for healing.

Physical benefits: Recommended for helping with dehydration or balanced water levels in body, excess water retention.

Emotional healing: Sometimes worn in pendants to heal heartbreak, bryozoan is comforting for loss of parents at an early age.

Chakra: Root.

Bryozoans are tiny organisms that grow permanently attached to stones or seaweed.
  They feed on phytoplankton with tiny tentacles in the water and act like a filter to the marine environment. This fossil is a stimulus to creativity, especially for painting or sculpture based in traditional styles or methods, and for writing historical fiction. Use as a focus for prayers or empowerments for clean water in parts of the world where there is drought or an unsanitary water supply.

Candle colour: *Grey.*
Fragrances: *Cypress, musk.*
Practical uses: *Can be worn to resist emotional pressure.*
Magical significance: *If you want to banish a bad habit, pass your hands anti-clockwise, a few centimetres above the crystal, saying, "May [name] move from my life with blessings, harming none." Light an incense stick.*
Divinatory meaning: *You may be finding it hard to quit a bad habit that is damaging your health; persevere as relief will come soon.*
Zodiac: *Capricorn.*
Empowerment: *I will not be shaken from my core beliefs and standards.*

ANTHRACITE

Type: Carbon.

Colours: Dark grey, similar to jet in appearance but very shiny even in the natural state and silvery in tumbled version.

Availability: Common.

Physical benefits: A grounding crystal, thought to be good for righting chemical imbalances in the body.

Emotional healing: Heals the scars of an emotionally cold childhood or controlling relationship in older life; calms hyperventilation, phobias or crippling social shyness.

Chakra: Root.

Keep with savings books when you are building up the deposit for a home, whether owned or rented accommodation. When you move in, transfer it to the place you pay your bills to continue to draw in money; anthracite guards against domestic accidents; good also to stop pets and children from being afraid of loud noises, fireworks and storms; store near a computer to find last-minute holidays and keep a piece near the photograph of an elderly relative or friend you worry about.

Candle colour: *Grey.*
Fragrances: *Cinnamon, ginger, patchouli.*
Practical uses: *Carry in a pocket when involved in physically dangerous activities to prevent accidents.*
Magical significance: *Keep in a red bag near the hearth, so you will have enough, food, fuel and clothes through the year. Replace at midnight on New Year's Eve and bury the old piece.*
Divinatory meaning: *Someone unwelcoming to you will display a softening of attitude.*
Zodiac: *Scorpio and Capricorn.*
Empowerment: *I attract and share abundance.*

CHIASTOLITE

Type: A form of andalusite.

Colours: Grey with black or brown equal-armed cross inclusion.

Availability: Obtainable from specialist crystal stores and online.

Physical benefits: May be beneficial for rheumatism and gout, nerve and muscle weakness and damage, mobility, strokes, paralysis.

Emotional healing: Can encourage slow but significant progress for people locked in destructive behaviour such as always choosing a faithless or abusive partner.

Chakra: Root.

Chiastolite comes from China and is unique.
  Associated in the modern world with Christianity, it is more anciently a symbol of the four cardinal points – north, east, south and west – and the central fusion of their energies. A chiastolite cross in the centre of your home will radiate life force in all directions and attract harmony and health. It is considered a bridge between dimensions, particularly in learning mediumship, practising spirit rescue or investigating a haunting, and it is also protective.

Candle colour: *Brown.*
Fragrances: *Almond, anise, bay, benzoin, clary sage.*
Practical uses: *Wear chiastolite jewellery or carry a stone with a clearly defined cross for international travel or if you work or live in any kind of trouble-spot.*
Magical significance: *Protects against all forms of malice: traditionally worn to repel the evil eye and against all paranormal harm.*
Divinatory meaning: *A time for choices and action, as doing nothing is not an option.*
Zodiac: *Capricorn.*
Empowerment: *I trust my judgement to make wise choices.*

METEORITE

Type: Magnetic space rock, alloyed with nickel and iron.

Colours: Grey, black, brown-black or red-brown on outside, often silver-grey inside.

Availability: Some rare, some relatively common.

Physical benefits: May help with muscle spasms, muscular tension, stomach cramps, digestive system; illness difficult to diagnose or treatment slow to show results, head or brain disorder, injury or pain, eye problems such as squints or cataracts, facial disfigurement.

Emotional healing: Keeps feet firmly on the ground when caught up in heady emotional attachments or sudden temptations later regretted.

Chakra: Root and Solar Plexus.

Candle colour: *Silver.*

Fragrances: *Frankincense, grapefruit, lime, myrrh, sandalwood.*

Practical uses: *Place meteorite around the home near entrances, to protect from fire or attack. Carry meteorite as an amulet against international terrorism, bombs, hijacking or violent crime, especially involving guns or knives.*

Magical significance: *A stone for those involved in astrology or cryptozoology; helpful for any who have experienced alien encounters in dreams or more directly.*

Divinatory meaning: *You may need to leave preconceptions behind when dealing with an unusual situation or person with a totally different life view.*

Zodiac: *All signs, especially Aquarius and Scorpio.*

Empowerment: *There is a whole universe of experience to be discovered.*

Most meteorites originate in the asteroid belt between Mars and Jupiter. The ancient Egyptians had a hieroglyph for meteorite that translates as heavenly metal, and capped some of their pyramids with them. The Black Stone at Mecca is a meteorite, believed in Islamic tradition to have been sent from Heaven to show Adam and Eve where to build the first temple.

Meteorites help to bring visions and messages from the cosmos to assist us to make the world a better place in small personal ways. Good for taking first steps towards a more fulfilling way of life, lifestyle change or even downsizing to attain a dream.

STIBNITE

Type: Antimony sulphide.

Colours: Metallic silver-grey lustre.

Availability: Obtainable through specialist crystal stores and online.

Physical benefits: Assists with disorders of the stomach, digestion, the oesophagus, and eases muscle spasm or tension; for improving reflexes and building bodily defences against infectious diseases, including new strains.

Emotional healing: By giving us courage, support and protection, stibnite assists us in relationship issues, particularly involving those who seek to control or suffocate our individuality.

Chakra: Brow and Crown.

Candle colour: *Grey.*
Fragrances: *Honeysuckle, rosemary, thyme.*
Practical uses: *Keep this crystal where natural light shines on it, even in winter, to draw in money from different sources and minimize demands on existing resources; a good anti-debt crystal, particularly if creditors are getting nasty.*
Magical significance: *Good for the return of lost, mislaid or stolen property or pets; set it on top of the name of items or photographs of a missing pet and picture the item or pet coming back.*
Divinatory meaning: *You suddenly regain the confidence to remove the influence of someone who tries to control you.*
Zodiac: *Scorpio and Capricorn.*
Empowerment: *I am strong and so I am protected.*

Stibnite offers concentrated focus during meditation if there is background noise or time is limited. Healers should hold a pendulum or crystal above a stibnite cluster to direct powers to roots of problems if these are uncertain. If asking a pendulum yes/no questions where truth is in question, hold it above stibnite for about a minute and then keep it there as you ask.

Stibnite is a truth crystal, and protects against mind games and intrusions into personal space or privacy. One near a computer deters both Internet hackers and the over-curious from trying to read private emails.

WARNING: Stibnite is toxic; wash hands after use, do not use in elixirs or ingest, and keep away from children and pets.

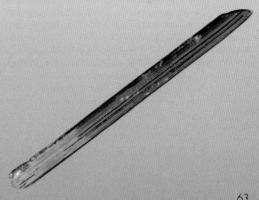

SILVER

Type: Metal.

Colours: Silver.

Availability: Common.

Physical benefits: Believed to help detoxification, digestion of essential elements, fertility, PMS, menstruation, pregnancy, hormones, migraines, speech and communication, fluid retention, circulation blockages, pineal and pituitary glands, wounds.

Emotional healing: Believed to assist women at every stage and age to value and care for their body; can be worn by men who have been forced into a macho role and all people who were inadequately mothered.

Chakra: Sacral.

Candle colour: *White or silver.*
Fragrances: *Eucalyptus, jasmine, lemon, myrrh, poppy.*
Practical uses: *Wearing silver jewellery attracts love, fertility and prosperity; silver doubles the powers of crystal jewellery. Crystals are most powerful and harmonious if in a silver wire cradle rather than drilled with a hole for a chain.*
Magical significance: *Lucky charms are traditionally silver: a key for a new home, a heart for love, a treasure chest for prosperity, a boat or plane for travel. Wear them on a bracelet or in a bag. Empower by leaving on an indoor window ledge all night at full moon.*
Divinatory meaning: *Minor financial luck is heading your way, but do not use it up helping someone who could manage.*
Zodiac: *Cancer.*
Empowerment: *I will trust my intuition and gut feelings.*

Silver, sacred to the moon, is energized by the waxing and full moon. Surround crystals and silver jewellery on the nights of crescent and full moons with a circle of lighted silver candles. Traditionally silver is turned over three times facing the crescent moon when it first appears to attract success in the month ahead.

 Silver is the crystal of love, especially new and young love or love after betrayal, and a powerful fertility symbol. Prick a moonstone or tiny rose-quartz egg with a silver-coloured pin or paper knife on the night of the full moon before making love. Leave the egg and knife open on an indoor window ledge all night. Then wrap them in white silk to incubate till the next full moon.

Iron Pyrites

Type: Iron sulphide.

Colours: Metallic and silvery.

Availability: Common.

Physical benefits: May be useful for colds, flu and other viral attacks, digestion, healing diseased bones, blood disorders especially red cell, anaemia, lung disorders.

Emotional healing: Very protective against ongoing control, criticism and manipulation by a partner, parent or employer, giving the power to resist without becoming angry or upset and so change the balance of power.

Chakra: Solar Plexus.

Iron pyrites contains hidden fire and the ability to generate wealth by one's own efforts. It has been given the name fool's gold, alluding to the fact that it has been mistaken for the more valuable material. However, real gold can sometimes be found adjacent to pyrites, so maybe the foolish person is one that does not follow the signs and omens life provides. Carry or wear pyrites as a protective amulet when you are away from home.
  WARNING: Do not use in elixirs or ingest.

Candle colour: *Gold or silver.*
Fragrances: *Copal, frankincense, ginger.*
Practical uses: *At home and work iron pyrites deters the user from making unwise financial decisions.*
Magical significance: *A large slab-like polished pyrite can be used as an excellent scrying mirror.*
Divinatory significance: *A seeming bargain arrives at the time most needed. It could be the answer, but check carefully.*
Zodiac: *Aries or Leo.*
Empowerment: *I accept only what is positive into my life.*

GALENA/GALENITE

Type: Lead sulphide.

Colours: Silver-grey, shimmering.

Availability: Common.

Physical benefits: Said to be useful for respiration, nervous system, inflammation, boils, abscesses and ulcers on the skin, circulation, veins, hair, infections, radiation (both to assist necessary treatment and to filter harmful waves from the world), problems of ageing, absorption of minerals, particularly zinc.

Emotional healing: Assists the newly grieving to feel the love of deceased friends and family even though the physical presence is gone; overcomes fears of personal mortality.

Chakra: Root.

Candle colour: *Silver.*

Fragrances: *Bistort, cypress, galbanum, mimosa, myrrh.*

Practical uses: *A symbol of transformation of what is old or redundant, a piece of galena melts limits imposed by self and eases the transition from one stage to another; encourages the newly separated to explore single life rather than rushing straight into a new relationship.*

Magical significance: *A piece of galena acts as a psychic shield if set where air flows all round, absorbing bad vibes, ill-wishing and free-floating negativity and transforming it into warmth, energy and optimism.*

Divinatory meaning: *Do not give up on a lost opportunity or blocked resources; the door will open.*

Zodiac: *Capricorn.*

Empowerment: *I shield myself from unwelcome energies.*

Galena has been used since 3000 BC as a lead-containing ore. Because galena often contains other minerals, especially silver, zinc and cadmium, and is found with beautiful crystals such as fluorite and marcasite, it has acquired metaphysical power to reveal hidden treasures. This includes the return of what was lost, stolen or rightfully yours, and the unexpected gift or acquisition of something as valuable in its place. Lead curse tablets were thrown by the ancient Romans into sacred waters to demand the return of stolen property.

   WARNING: Toxic due to lead content and other minerals. Do not use to make direct elixirs or let children or animals touch it.

Black Star Diopside

Type: Pyroxene, calcium magnesium silicate or calcium iron silicate (see also green diopside).

Colours: Dark brown to dark greenish black and black, with four-rayed star that can be seen when cut and polished in dome-shaped cabochons but lost in faceting; alternatively sometimes found as cat's eye.

Availability: Rare, but beautiful and worth obtaining.

Physical benefits: May help back, slipped discs, lumbago, spine, skeleton, back of the neck, muscle strains and spasms, ligaments, bowels, anus, large intestine, prostate, hernia, knees and feet, chronic constipation, kidneys, fluid blockages, chronic pain.

Emotional healing: Called the stone of healing tears, black diopside releases sorrows and grief that have become blocked, liberating for men who have been told it is unmanly to express softer emotions and cry.

Chakra: Root.

Candle colour: *Dark green.*
Fragrances: *Cypress, lemon balm, mugwort, myrrh, tea tree.*
Practical uses: *Black diopside in its natural form is a very calming crystal for hyperactive, aggressive or traumatized pets.*
Magical significance: *The star in black diopside acts a gateway to other dimensions; shine a narrow torch beam on the star or angle the diopside star so that candlelight illuminates it; in your mind travel inwards to a point of light that expands as a golden doorway in your inner vision; also for making wishes under a starry sky.*
Divinatory meaning: *Express your feelings of frustration at the uncooperative attitude by someone who is thwarting your efforts, or the situation may continue indefinitely.*
Zodiac: *Pisces.*
Empowerment: *What I feel is valid and should not be denied.*

Black star diopside is called the Black Star of India as that is where it is mostly found. It is the only crystal to produce a four- instead of six-rayed white star; this distinguishes it from the similar black star sapphire.
  A dual-energy gem, it enhances creativity and at the same time encourages logic and analysis. Black diopside in its natural form softens stubborn attitudes and is equally effective for toddlers and temperamental adults; encourages over-conservative partners and older relatives to try new things.

AEGERINE

Type: Sodium iron silicate.

Colours: Black or dark green or brownish black.

Availability: Available from specialist crystal stores or online.

Physical benefits: Seen as useful to help boost immune system and trigger self-healing; good for general healing, to overcome insomnia and sleep disturbances, a natural energizer.

Emotional healing: Believed to assist in mending a broken heart after betrayal or loss; overcome a sense of being overwhelmed by life and responsibilities, relieve depression, self-consciousness and unnecessary shame over appearance and so good if a person has any disfigurement or body image problems.

Chakra: Root and Solar Plexus.

Named after the Norse sea deity, Aegir, since it was first found close to the sea in Norway.

A stone of particular benefit in Reiki or any other energy-transference healing systems using the power of touch. Aegerine helps acceptance of what cannot be changed and also of yourself and others as they are. Use aegerine to defy outdated convention to follow your own path or stand up for what you know is right.

Take aegirine on journeys of self-discovery, whether spiritual or travelling to see far-off places; good for backpackers to protect them against negative energies and inhospitable places and people.

Candle colour: *Dark green.*
Fragrances: *Apple blossom, honeysuckle, rose, thyme, violet.*
Practical uses: *Generates enthusiasm and a team spirit at; encourages teenagers to get out of bed in the morning.*
Magical significance: *Powerfully protective if you are suffering jealousy, malice or psychological or psychic attack from others; once a week use the rod shape as a wand and thrust it away from you in all directions as you hold it in the hand you write with, saying, "May none penetrate this shield of protection."*
Divinatory meaning: *Someone is trying to make you feel inadequate or guilty to offload their own insecurities and hang-ups, so do not accept blame or guilt.*
Zodiac: *Pisces.*
Empowerment: *I will remain true to my own principles whatever the pressures.*

BLACK CORAL

Colours: Organic, branching calcareous skeletons of sea creatures that can be highly polished and shine translucent as crystals or jewellery.

Availability: One of the rarer corals.

Physical benefits: Alleged to be a natural pain reliever, absorb energies from acute illnesses, fever and infections, improve functioning of bowels, spine and spinal fluid, bones; and to be good for blood-cell enrichment; absorption of iodine, the alimentary canal, thalamus, balance in older people, male potency.

Emotional healing: A soothing crystal to wear if a partner dies, particularly in the early years of marriage; also assists grieving parents who lose a child at any age.

Chakra: Root.

Candle colour: *Dark grey or purple.*
Fragrances: *Cypress, lemon balm, mugwort, myrrh, sweetgrass.*
Practical uses: *Use as a household protector and luck bringer. Touch every door to the house and individual rooms, on each handle on both sides, with a branch of coral; then hang the coral inside over the front door to filter the energies of those entering.*
Magical significance: *Called king's coral, in ancient times black coral could only be worn by kings who were believed to be divinely chosen and so had healing powers; hence black coral enhances wisdom and healing abilities. Wear if learning a spiritual tradition such as Buddhism, Druidry or Reiki.*
Divinatory meaning: *Keep a low profile and listen rather than speak until you are sure what the intentions of others are.*
Zodiac: *Pisces.*
Empowerment: *I will use my gifts for the right reasons.*

Though mainly associated with Hawaii, where black coral is the official US state gemstone, coral in Ancient Egypt was ground and mixed with seeds and scattered on the ground after the Nile flood receded to bring fertility to the land. Black coral was sacred to Osiris, the corn and vegetation god: black was a colour of fertility.

Its name in Arabic means ease or well-being, and black coral is said to bring serenity to the wearer, absorbing negativity. It needs cleaning with incense regularly. Black coral is not so suitable for children.

Some ecologists only use coral that has naturally broken off, not been cut or harvested. Black coral protects against bad weather, particularly hurricanes, typhoons, high winds, floods and tsunamis.

BLACK KYANITE

Type: Aluminium silicate.

Colours: Steel grey or black.

Availability: Rarer than blue kyanite, but available from some specialist crystal stores or online.

Physical benefits: Alleged to be useful for adrenal glands, reducing blood pressure, pain relief, vocal cords, bone marrow, sickle cell, neurological disorders, visual disturbances.

Emotional healing: Absorbs panic and inability to switch off negative cycles of thoughts; helps us to forget what we cannot resolve, whether a bitter divorce or someone who was unkind to us dying without reconciliation.

Chakra: Root.

Favoured by energy healers for cleansing the aura energy field and the energies of a room after healing; pass diagonally up and down the body to clear the inner chakra power system. Circle over the hairline and round head and shoulders to mend tears in the aura.
  Stimulates psychic energies, but protects beginners from frightening psychic phenomena. Move vertically down the body to close your psychic energies after a session or still yourself. A dream crystal that will enable you to travel safely in sleep to other dimensions.

Candle colour: *Silver.*
Fragrances: *Anise, galbanum, mugwort, myrrh, thyme.*
Practical uses: *Keep blades pointing outwards on indoor window ledges to deflect incoming tensions and disperse emotions.*
Magical significance: *Point individual blades away from you to deflect harm and towards you while naming what you need.*
Divinatory meaning: *Something thought wrong for you is returning and is now right.*
Zodiac: *Aquarius and Pisces.*
Empowerment: *The stars fill me with inspiration.*

MELANITE GARNET

Type: Calcium iron silicate, andradite variety of garnet.

Colours: Black, glossy and shiny.

Availability: Relatively rare.

Physical benefits: Believed to assist with pain relief, bones, rheumatism, arthritis, bowels, colon, constipation, anus, testes, male sexual dysfunction, prostate, hernia, absorption of medication while minimizing side-effects, blood particularly red cells and iron deficiency, strokes, heart attacks, considered helpful for cancers of lower half of body, liver, infections, immune system, moles and melanomas anywhere on the body.

Emotional healing: Often called the male-focus garnet, good for men whose feelings are locked, maybe due to stern fathering or a strict single-sex school, and who find it hard to express love or enjoy spontaneous pleasure.

Chakra: Root.

Candle colour: *Grey.*

Fragrances: *Anise, dragon's blood, musk, mugwort, sage.*

Practical uses: *A dual-focus crystal for resolving relationship issues in a practical way with the minimum of hurt and blame; wearing one will either lead you to reconciliation or, if this is not possible, assist you in gentle parting; it also absorbs unnecessary guilt and grounds you in the real situation if a partner is trying to offload their bad behaviour as your fault.*

Magical significance: *One of the best protective crystals against black magic, curses, hexes or a sense of menace.*

Divinatory meaning: *Stay in the here-and-now and defeat immediate problems rather than jumping ahead to future hazards or triumphs not yet in sight.*

Zodiac: *Capricorn.*

Empowerment: *I am totally rooted in reality.*

Melanite is the most earth-related garnet and is worn by men and women to draw strength from the earth for practical endeavours and starting ventures from the roots upwards; ensures any creation is based on firm foundations. An excellent domestic room cleanser, melanite absorbs anything that is not fresh and pure.

Natural black garnet on a matrix (rock or crystal base) should be worn if you live with head-in-the-clouds people; give melanite to a partner who forgets to pay household bills or fill in necessary forms.

JET

Type: Organic: fossilized wood that has been turned into a dense form of coal called lignite.

Colours: Black, very dark brown, glassy.

Availability: Common.

Physical benefits: Considered helpful for headache, migraines, epilepsy, swollen glands, colds, labour pains, menstrual cramps, toothache, neuralgia, stomach pains caused by irritations of the colon or bowel and colds.

Emotional healing: Overcomes grief and depression after bereavement, especially after the death of a partner, and conquers negative thought patterns or fears of others doing harm or sending bad luck even if unfounded.

Chakra: Root.

Jet has been used since ancient times in association with death and protection against evil entities, having been discovered in prehistoric burial chambers.

Used by Viking women in spindles to sew with magical chants to protect their husbands' garments, jet was also carried by sailors' wives in Europe as an amulet to keep their husbands safe at sea – and faithful. Carved ornate jet jewellery was made popular in mourning by Queen Victoria, while jet crosses were worn around the neck to repel evil witches and the powers of darkness. Traditionally, jet should be buried with its owner and not resold or inherited. If it is handed on, wash weekly for three weeks and dry outdoors.

Candle colour: *Black, natural beeswax or dark brown.*
Fragrances: *Cypress, galbanum, mimosa, myrrh, patchouli.*
Practical uses: *For those that live with relatives who suffer depression or psychological illness, place pieces of jet around the home, especially in the area where they spend most of their time, to absorb negative energies. Smudge the jet weekly with the smoke of jet-fragrance incense.*
Magical significance: *Worn around the neck, jet acts as a shield against envy, jealousy, ill wishing, spiteful words and psychic attack, whether from human or paranormal source.*
Divinatory meaning: *Financial stability will come unexpectedly as a result of earlier hard work and input you thought had been unsuccessful.*
Zodiac: *Capricorn.*
Empowerment: *I can let go of the past with gentleness.*

SPHALERITE

Type: Zinc sulphide in crystalline form, the chief ore of zinc, and almost always containing some iron.

Colours: Black, dark grey, red, brown and yellow.

Availability: Obtainable from specialist crystal stores or online; clear is rarer.

Physical benefits: Thought to assist with problems with women's reproductive system, male genitals and sperm count, increased libido, vitality, immune system, infections, extremities of temperature, fevers or hypothermia.

Emotional healing: A grounding stone if someone loves too much or mistakes indiscriminate sex for affection; resolving gender and same-sex-partnership issues; bi-polar disorder.

Chakra: Solar Plexus, Sacral and Root.

Candle colour: *Dark grey or indigo.*
Fragrances: *Almond, bergamot, lavender, lily of the valley, peppermint.*
Practical uses: *Keep close when you need extra energy.*
Magical significance: *Allows you to make sense of psychic messages during divination or channelling and intuitive thought, especially if you are naturally logical or new to spiritual work.*
Divinatory meaning: *You cannot please everyone, so consider what you want regardless of whom it offends.*
Zodiac: *Gemini and Scorpio.*
Empowerment: *I make my own choices and stick with them.*

As well as its grounding properties, sphalerite can act as a wake-up call, usually if we have rooted ourselves in a situation that is not as stable as it appears.The black variety, known as black jack, has a higher iron content than the other colours and is very grounding.

  In contrast, the red crystals, known as ruby jack, have very little or no iron content and will bring change, inventiveness and independence. A crystal of truth; meditate or hold sphalerite to tell reality from illusion or deception; protects against treachery.

BLACK TIGER'S EYE

Type: Quartz embedded in crocidolite with little of the hydrated oxide that gives tiger's eye its customary golden colour; very dark form of hawk's or falcon's eye (blue).

Colours: Black or very dark blue, also includes darker greys, sometimes dyed.

Availability: Rarest form of tiger's eye.

Physical benefits:: May help all slow-moving degenerative conditions, to trigger the body's natural resistance, deep-seated tumours or growths anywhere, prostate, hernia, bowels, large intestine and anus, internal bleeding, deep vein thrombosis, mental and physical blackouts.

Emotional healing: A stone for men who have suffered a severe setback, such as the loss of a lifetime partner, redundancy and no prospect of re-employment or a financial disaster, to work through and rebuild their lives step by step in a new way.

Chakra: Root.

This very unusual tiger's eye is much heavier in its energies than its brother the hawk's or falcon's eye. Even if dyed, it maintains its gleaming exterior and is sometimes called the impenetrable fortress stone; the best stone for allowing anything unhelpful to bounce back with triple the force it was sent with and for galvanizing your defences.

Black tiger's eye is both empowering and protective for anyone in the armed forces, to focus on their strengths and loyalties to one another. Give black tiger's eye to any woman who has to walk home alone at night or lives alone in a troubled area, to remain calm and exude personal power.

Associated candle colour: *Dark grey.*

Associated fragrances: *Anise, cloves, grapefruit, lime, tea tree.*

Practical uses: *Wear black tiger's-eye jewellery at the most difficult times to give you the sheer doggedness and stubbornness not to give in to adversity or bullying; touch the jewellery in the darkest hours to push towards the light at the end of the tunnel.*

Magical significance: *The ultimate defensive shield to reflect back hostility and protect you. If you know you will be meeting a draining or nasty person, touch your brow, your throat and your heat with the stone to seal your chakra weak-points.*

Divinatory meaning: *If the odds seem stacked against you, keep pushing, as a week or two will see you through.*

Zodiac: *Scorpio.*

Empowerment: *I overcome adversity with courage.*

HEALER'S GOLD

Type: Pyrite and magnetite combined.

Colours: Black with gold (sometimes white inclusions) or black and silver.

Availability: Relatively rare but worth obtaining.

Physical benefits: Allows healers to work with patients without becoming depleted; believed to assist with blood conditions, circulation, bowels, intestines, excessive bleeding, blood clots, pain relief, exhaustion from illness or treatment.

Emotional healing: Protects against all who drain energy and from emotionally draining situations.

Chakra: Solar Plexus.

Attracts what is needed and keeps away unhelpful energies. Light white candles round a natural piece in your central downstairs room; ask blessings on all departed spirits and request that they either remain in peace and love or depart. Leave candles burning and when they are burned down, open the nearest window. A stone of fidelity and love. Hang a pendant over the bed with sprigs of dried rosemary in a drawstring bag; replace the herbs monthly and scatter them. Smudge monthly with a frankincense or myrrh incense stick spiralled over it, asking that you remain together in fidelity and love.

Candle colour: *Gold.*
Fragrances: *Chamomile, copal, cyphi, myrrh.*
Practical uses: *A stabilizing crystal that attracts good fortune; a natural piece restores normality after a crisis, eases grief and assists in rebuilding.*
Magical significance: *Enhances spiritual healing, also for practitioners of conventional medicine to channel energy from the earth to act as a conductor of healing and to shield patients from harmful effects of equipment or drugs.*
Divinatory meaning: *A creative period to attract the necessary resources through hard work and by making tough decisions to shed what is working against you.*
Zodiac: *Leo.*
Empowerment: *I have the strength to resist pressure.*

LARVAKITE

Type: Black feldspar.

Colours: Black-grey, blue-grey, grey, all with sheen or iridescent colour flashes, often of silvery blue.

Availability: Found in specialist crystal stores and online.

Physical benefits: Said to help high blood pressure, brain functioning, recovery after strokes and thrombosis, brain stem, intellect, congested lungs, PMS, menopausal hot flushes, skin.

Emotional healing: Encourages rationality; ideal for hormonal teenagers, pregnancy, perimenopausal mood swings and passionate new lovers.

Chakra: Base, Throat, Brow, Crown.

Candle colour: *Blue or silver.*

Fragrances: *Myrrh, poppy, rosemary, sage, sweetgrass.*

Practical uses: *Carry if you are learning new skills; you have to combine learning with work or caring for a family, if you are under financial pressure or face opposition to your studies.*

Magical significance: *Reverses spells; wear to neutralize nasty wishes and consign them to the cosmos for transformation.*

Divinatory meaning: *Do not part with money unless you are sure the person asking has a genuine need and will pay you back.*

Zodiac: *Leo and Sagittarius.*

Empowerment: *I open my heart wisely.*

Larvikite, or Norwegian moonstone, is an igneous rock that is mined in Norway, named after the local town of Larvik. It is useful for activating those with grand dreams who are going to start tomorrow. Larvikite has grounding energies to connect with nature and counteract over-exposure to artificial stimulants, over-bright lighting and constant background noise. It brings psychic dreams, connecting with ancestors, spirit guides and past lives, and aids recall and understanding of dream messages. Brings healing during sleep.

LILAC KUNZITE

Type: Silicate/spodumene.

Colours: Lavender, violet and purple.

Availability: Less common than pink, but available from specialist crystal stores and online.

Physical benefits: Believed to help relieve menopausal symptoms of all kinds and for older women to resolve gynaecological problems that reduce libido; protect against chemical pollutants, also memory loss.

Emotional healing: Prompts acceptance that a former partner does not want to be with you, the need to constantly have company, also schizophrenia.

Chakra: Brow.

Candle colour: *Lilac.*

Fragrances: *Lavender, lilac, magnolia, violet.*

Practical uses: *Keep kunzite in the car to ease tension of driving, also to counteract road rage.*

Magical significance: *Increases intuitive powers; a good channel through which to increase awareness of spiritual guardians.*

Divinatory meaning: *Think carefully before an expensive purchase.*

Zodiac: *Pisces and Taurus.*

Empowerment: *I do not need to spend money to be happy.*

Keep all kunzite out of sunlight, as it fades. Because kunzite does splinter and because of the nature of the stone, you will rarely find flawless gems, but kunzite jewellery has a healing power that more expensive gems sometimes lack.

Wear lilac kunzite to attract a partner who is open to life's adventures. Lilac kunzite protects against harmful spirits. Carry lilac kunzite if you are visiting a house where an unhappy event has occurred.

BLUE LACE AGATE

Type: Oxide, cryptocrystalline quartz.

Colours: Pale blue, sometimes brighter blue with white or even brown threads of colour.

Availability: Common.

Physical benefits: Thought to relieve sore throats and aching or swollen glands in the neck by soaking a crystal in water for eight hours, removing crystal and gargling; also to be good for thyroid problems, high blood pressure and soothing skin allergiesand tension-related headaches.

Emotional healing: Calms stress-related conditions and communication difficulties.

Chakra: Throat.

In pre-Christian times in Scandinavia and Denmark, blue lace agate was dedicated to Nerthus the earth mother. Carry or wear blue lace agate to improve your communicative abilities, if you struggle to express your emotions without getting upset. Will also lower the volume of communication, so keep a bowl of crystals in the home if you have noisy children, a howling dog or screeching cat. Put blue lace agate on pictures of armed forces personnel you know to keep them safe.

Fragrances: *Fern, lavender, star anise, vervain, vetivert, yarrow.*
Practical uses: *Protects those who help others or who act as carers for the disabled, sick or very old; also for parents of small children, to give them patience.*
Magical significance: *Assists you to hear the words of your guardian angel by activating your psychic hearing abilities.*
Divinatory meaning: *Express the feelings that are in your heart honestly and you will receive a favourable response.*
Zodiac: *Aquarius.*
Empowerment: *I speak the truth with kindness.*

BLUE CORAL

Type: Organic, branching calcareous skeletons of sea creatures.

Colours: Light to mid blue with white spots or smudges.

Availability: Relatively common.

Physical benefits: Said to promote the speedy healing of fractured bones; relieve rashes, acne, burns, high blood pressure, recurring seasonal illnesses such as hay fever, sunburn, sunstroke; help balance minerals in body.

Emotional healing: Helpful for women during or after the menopause to overcome fears of lack of desirability and to welcome the serenity of growing older.

Chakra: Throat.

Blue coral is sacred to Diwata ng Dagat, the goddess of the sea in the Philippines, one of the main areas from which blue coral comes. When worn as jewellery, many women find it gives them a calm strength in daily life and that it counteracts PMS.

Men also relate well to blue coral as it brings out an ability to let go of irritations. Keep as blue tumblestones in your home if you have small children, to protect them from water-related hazards.

Candle colour: *Blue.*

Fragrances: *Kelp, lavender, lemon, lotus.*

Practical uses: *Protects travellers, especially those who travel by boat.*

Magical significance: *Light blue candles in the bathroom, play dolphin sounds and lie in your bath holding blue coral, to relax totally.*

Divinatory meaning: *You may disagree strongly with someone's opinion, but now is not the time to speak out; wait and the opportunity will come to turn matters your way.*

Zodiac: *Pisces.*

Empowerment: *I do not fear being carried by the tides of life.*

COVELLITE

Type: Copper sulphide, minor ore of copper.

Colours: Almost black, indigo blue or midnight blue, with a blue metallic iridescence.

Availability: Rare but obtainable from some specialist crystal stores and online.

Physical benefits: Considered good for ears, eyes, throat, sinuses, mouth, cellular disorders; helpful in cancer treatment; helpful when diagnosis or prognosis is uncertain or treatment is causing bad side effects.

Emotional healing: For anyone with or living with a person with an inflated ego, to get in touch with reality.

Chakra: Throat and Brow.

Candle colour: *Dark blue.*
Fragrances: *Cedar, cyphi, sandalwood, ylang ylang.*
Magical significance: *The best stone to hold during rebirthing, where a therapist guides you back through your own birth process to overcome blind spots.*
Divinatory meaning: *One of those times when the greater good has to take priority over personal desires; in the longer term this will benefit you.*
Zodiac: *Libra and Sagittarius.*
Empowerment: *I can wait a little longer for fulfilment.*

Covellite, sometimes called covelline, is regarded as a crystal of small miracles to turn dreams into reality and bring hope where there is none, combining Earthly effort with what is sometimes called divine intervention.

Wear it as you remind yourself of the success that is coming, and to overcome a period of despondency or acute anxiety. Use also in healing or psychic work if there are blocks, or if knowledge is getting in the way of spiritual insight and messages.

BLUE QUARTZ

Type: Silicon dioxide, clear quartz that contains various inclusions which give the blue colour.

Colours: Pale to mid blue, or as bright cobalt blue in artificially grown Siberian quartz.

Availability: Depends on type of blue quartz.

Physical benefits: Blue quartz is maintained to strengthen the immune system, thyroid, throat, glands, spleen, hay fever, absorption of minerals, heat stroke, sunburn and burns.

Emotional healing: Assists those who absorb hurtful behaviour by others into themselves rather than speaking out, so creating stress that manifests as physical symptoms.

Chakra: Throat.

Candle colour: *Blue*
Fragrances: *Eucalyptus, lavender, lilac, tea tree.*
Practical uses: *Soothes excitable adults and children.*
Magical significance: *Helps develop mediumship abilities.*
Divinatory meaning: *You may feel overwhelmed by work, but this will pass if you take time for yourself.*
Zodiac: *Libra.*
Empowerment: *I find fulfilment in doing things well.*

All blue quartz brings harmony and order to chaotic situations and people and clarity to muddled thinking; excellent therefore for sorting accounts or creating organized and focused reports or proposals. It is very lucky for anyone trying to make a career in music and is a power stone for music lovers, from rock to opera.
  Blue quartz enhances the effect of reciting prayer beads, chanting mantras, singing sacred songs or listening to religious music.

BLUE KYANITE

Type: Aluminium silicate.

Colours: Blue to blue-green, striated, sometimes streaked with black; can be shiny, almost pearly, sometimes with white.

Availability: Rare in transparent gem quality, but more common in other forms.

Physical benefits: Said to promote mobility, cells, tissues, bone marrow, throat, voice, neurological system; assist with strokes particularly with improvement in speech and mobility, blockages and constrictions anywhere in the body.

Emotional healing: Brings tranquillity as a result of breaking free from emotional blackmail, possessiveness and self-imposed guilt.

Chakra: Throat and Brow.

Candle colour: *Blue.*

Fragrances: *Bergamot, cedar, iris, juniper, peppermint.*

Practical uses: *If your child does not get asked to parties or is ignored in play parks, keep bladed kyanite near their outdoor or school clothes at home to make them more popular; helpful if your child is physically different in any way or has difficulty in integrating.*

Magical significance: *Hold blue kyanite and ask aloud for your heart's desire, from the first day of the month till the next first of the month. On the second, leave your kyanite where someone else can find it to pass on luck.*

Divinatory meaning: *You will have cause to speak your mind. But do not waste words on those who will not listen.*

Zodiac: *Pisces.*

Empowerment: *I understand my life's purpose.*

If you have lost your way in life or are doing totally the wrong thing, create an empowerment grid by laying out rows of small kyanite blades on a table radiating from a central kyanite in six different directions.

Each night, touch and walk in your mind a different kyanite path from the centre, letting images and ideas appear spontaneously; start with the first row you set. After six days, wait a day and begin again, repeating the row sequence until you are back on track and no longer need the grid.

Blue kyanite, like black, does not accumulate or store negative energies and, along with citrine, these are the only crystals that do not require cleansing.

Shattuckite

Type: Copper silicate.

Colours: Deep blue, turquoise-blue, sometimes with azure or brown streaks.

Availability: Relatively rare, but obtainable from specialist crystal stores and online.

Physical benefits: Thought to help with ear, nose and throat, particularly infections and inflammations such as swollen glands, tonsillitis, mouth, tooth and gum disorders, coagulation of blood, arthritic and rheumatic conditions.

Emotional healing: Releases within you the need to hold on to the past – especially useful in getting over a relationship breakdown or waiting for someone who will never commit.

Chakra: Throat and Brow.

Shattuckite was a traditional magical healing and love charm among indigenous people in Arizona and parts of Africa. Use shattuckite to enable you to interpret information and wisdom you receive and to protect you from feeling threatened by entities from other dimensions during channelling or mediumship. Shattuckite can resolve past-life issues that prevent you from moving forward in present-life spiritual development and help you to bring back strengths and strategies from past worlds to assist in present-day dilemmas.

Candle colour: *Blue.*
Fragrances: *Cherry blossom, copal.*
Practical uses: *Enables those in love to reveal their feelings.*
Magical significance: *To improve your automatic writing, hold shattuckite in the hand you do not write with and a green-ink pen in the other. Words will flow on to the paper from your angels.*
Divinatory meaning: *Time to say goodbye to the past rather than waiting for what you know will never happen.*
Zodiac: *Aquarius.*
Empowerment: *I can share my deepest feelings with those I love.*

FALCON/HAWK'S EYE

Type: Quartz embedded in crocidolite with a little of the hydrated oxide that gives tiger's eye its golden colour.

Colours: Blues, gleaming, also green-greys (stones like green tiger's eye are sometimes called cat's eye).

Availability: Relatively common.

Physical benefits: Considered beneficial for circulation, cholesterol, long-distance sight, sore throat, pharynx, laryngitis, sinuses, nasal congestion, motion sickness especially by air, medical tests, chemotherapy.

Emotional healing: Hypochondria and excessive terror of harm to or death of healthy loved ones; self-limiting behaviour.

Chakra: Throat.

Use when meditating in sunlight outdoors to reach a tranquil state of mind and guide you into spiritual realms for visions and insights of a personal or even global nature. A crystal that tells you instantly by its feel if someone is lying.

Place hawk's eye on your Brow chakra and relax for a few minutes to bring a new state of calm, when you are feeling stressed. Good for remote viewing, i.e. seeing people and places beyond the range of the physical eye, for clairvoyance and for out-of-body or mind travel.

Candle colour: *Blue.*
Fragrances: *Agrimony, anise, honeysuckle.*
Practical uses: *Safe travel, especially when backpacking and by air.*
Magical significance: *Hawk or falcon's eye is a charm against ill-wishing; especially from people we may not know are feeling malicious towards us, such as a jealous ex-lover.*
Divinatory meaning: *A sudden intuitive insight into a situation will overcome a problem where logic has failed.*
Zodiac: *Sagittarius.*
Empowerment: *I can travel in my mind to where I most wish to be.*

BLUE BARITE

Type: Sulphate, very soft.

Colours: Pale blue crystals.

Availability: Found in specialist crystal stores and online.

Physical benefits: Believed to assist with lowering blood pressure; soothing fevers, stress-related throat disorders; pain relief; protect against effects of radiotherapy and prolonged chemotherapy; good for physical shock; for mother and baby after a prolonged birth or one where there was surgical intervention.

Emotional healing: Releases blocked feelings and words that prevent you from sharing your deeper emotions.

Chakra: Throat.

Blue barite is a stone for healing the earth and the skies; helpful for global warming and the ozone layer; a crystal of self-sufficiency, it motivates you to live in a more ecologically sound way. A good stone for anyone in a war zone. Will give you confidence to live life your own way and to teach your children ethics so they can make wise decisions. Blue barite in a home can help a couple to make reasoned decisions. Each person should hold the crystal and be allowed to speak while the other must listen without comment, awaiting their own turn.

Candle colour: *Pale blue.*
Fragrances: *Bluebell, lily of the valley, vanilla, violet, wisteria.*
Practical uses: *Allows you to speak confidently when you must address a number of people or negotiate with an official.*
Magical significance: *Stimulates clairaudience so hold with closed eyes and listen to words that come into your mind.*
Divinatory meaning: *Listen to what is being said by someone opposing you. You will discover you are both saying the same thing in different ways.*
Zodiac: *Libra and Aquarius*
Empowerment: *I am not afraid to hear the truth.*

BENITOITE

Type: Cyclosilicate/barium titanium silicate.

Colours: Blue, purplish blue, some with white bands, sometimes colourless or yellowish, fluorescent.

Availability: Relatively rare, but very beautiful.

Physical benefits: May assist with mobility, joints, muscles, ligaments, throat problems, eyesight, glaucoma, insomnia, nightmares, cosmetic or plastic surgery, liposuction, Botox, any beautifying surgery or treatment, burns, scalds, high blood pressure, fevers, skin inflammation, scarring.

Emotional healing: Brings love of self, self-belief and improved body image; for all who have been rejected because of their physical appearance or a disfigurement, to know their true value.

Chakra: Throat.

Candle colour: *Blue.*
Fragrances: *Lilac, lotus, orchid, poppy, sandalwood.*
Practical uses: *A great joy-bringer that encourages the user to make the most of every moment; wear benitoite jewllery when you attend any social event.*
Magical significance: *Benitoite, especially when used with moldavite, enhances astral travel.*
Divinatory meaning: *A time for inspired ideas and the means to put them into practice.*
Zodiac: *Sagittarius.*
Empowerment: *I enjoy every new day and experience.*

Benetoite was originally thought to be a form of blue sapphire because of its intense blue colour when it was discovered in 1906. However, the crystals are small, and are in fact a rare mineral associated with the equally rare neptunite and natrolite. Wear benetoite for launching plans and for activity holidays such as rock-climbing or pot-holing. Benetoite inspires natural courage but not foolhardiness; helps overcome the fears of pushing yourself to the limits.

CHRYSOCOLLA

Type: Hydrated copper silicate. Gem silica is chrysocolla agatized in chalcedony quartz.

Colours: Mixed blues and bluish greens; occasionally turquoise.

Availability: Common.

Physical benefits: Maintained to be beneficial for digestion, hip joints and hip replacement, arthritis, rheumatism, metabolism, PMS, painful menstruation, foetal health, labour pains, thyroid, high blood pressure, blood sugar levels, diabetes particularly Type 2, blood disorders, lungs.

Emotional healing: Helps men to show their vulnerable feelings and aids in the recovery from violence by partners of either gender.

Chakra: Heart and Throat.

Chrysocolla is the stone of wise women, to help express knowledge and experience through writing, painting, music, crafts or acting; give it to grandmothers and great-grandmothers to help them balance caring with their need for independence; good for older people who feel nervous if living alone.

Chrysocolla is also the symbol of musicians; use as a charm to learn new musical instruments or to join a choir, orchestra or theatre group. It is excellent for people of any age who act childishly, to bring maturity without losing spontaneity; hide the stone in the luggage or glove box of a partner who is undergoing a mid-life crisis or has a roaming eye.

Candle colour: *Turquoise.*
Fragrances: *Lily, lotus, orchid, vanilla, violet.*
Practical uses: *A protective stone against obstructive neighbours, malice via computer or mobile phone, or spiteful remarks about age or physical appearance by creating a reverse energy force field that makes attackers feel shame.*
Magical significance: *For world peace, create a chrysocolla grid: set a circle of very small chrysocolla round a picture of world leaders meeting together, with four rows of chrysocolla radiating from a larger chrysocolla in the middle of the picture, touching the circle at the four compass points.*
Divinatory meaning: *You may need to be generous to someone you dislike to avoid hurting their feelings.*
Zodiac: *Taurus*
Empowerment: *I can use my life experiences to guide others.*

BLUE FLUORITE

Type: Halide, calcium fluoride.

Colours: Blue, either single colour or banded or as Blue John typically dark-blue/blue-purple and yellow banded.

Availability: Relatively rare.

Physical benefits: Seen as good for the immune system, inflammation and infection of the throat, bedwetting, earache and infections, improved speech after an accident, brain trauma or illness, Alzheimer's and senile dementia.

Emotional healing: The best stone for those who find it hard to accept everyday reality, to open up channels of communication.

Chakra: Throat and Brow.

The most famous blue fluorite, Blue John, a zoned or banded fluorite, is found only near Castleton in Derbyshire, England, and has at least 14 different banded or veined varieties. The Blue John colouring, a variety of banded blue-purples, greys and yellows, was created naturally by exposure to oily films millions of years ago. Good for resolving official or legal matters that have been slow-moving or delayed; helps children to distinguish between fantasy and truth. Place on base of your throat and on your brow to encourage clairaudience and clairvoyance.

Candle colour: *Blue or purple.*
Fragrances: *Hyacinth, honeysuckle, lavender, lilac, wisteria.*
Practical uses: *Blue fluorite is a stone of gentle honesty in all dealings; carry with you to soften dealings with those who are brutally frank.*
Magical Significance: *Hold single colour blue fluorite while cloud scrying.*
Divinatory meaning: *You are right to question the motives of someone unduly secretive. Be cautious*
Zodiac: *Pisces*
Empowerment: *I will speak honestly without giving hurt.*

BLUE SAPPHIRE

Type: Corundum (aluminium oxide).

Colours: Pale to midnight blue.

Availability: High quality is rare, but lower and non-gem quality more common.

Physical benefits: Reported to help thyroid, nervous system, blood disorders, dementia, degenerative diseases, ear infections, hearing, eyesight and eye infections, fevers, swollen glands, nausea, speech and communication.

Emotional healing: Helps to release spiritual and emotional blockages, allowing you to express your true self and needs and open to love.

Chakra: Throat.

Candle colour: *Blue.*

Fragrances: *Lemon balm, lemon verbena, lily, lotus, orchid.*

Practical uses: *Sapphire is a stone of love, commitment and fidelity, popular in betrothal rings. Twin matching sapphire tumblestones can be given to a couple moving in together or marrying; collect one for each year you are together.*

Magical significance: *Blue sapphire is considered effective for channelling healing powers and is popular with Reiki healers. Sapphire amplifies healing through the voice.*

Divinatory meaning: *You are wondering whether to trust someone you have recently met. Take your time as you do not know the whole story yet.*

Zodiac: *Virgo and Libra.*

Empowerment: *Truth is the key to trust and trust the key to truth.*

King Solomon's fabulous magical ring was said to have been a blue sapphire, a symbol of wisdom. The Ancient Greeks called the sapphire the jewel of the sun god Apollo. The blue stone was worn when consulting Apollo's oracle at Delphi so that the questioner might have the wisdom to understand the answer.

Blue sapphire, especially the velvety blue cornflower, also known as Kashmir, is the most desired and valuable sapphire. It offers calming, healing energies to all who wear or hold it, and will bring good luck. Sapphire helps during times of change to maintain a vision of where you want go and how to get there.

Sapphires are a symbol of integrity, a counterbalance to cynicism and less desirable aspects of modern culture; effective for resolution of judicial matters.

89

BLUE ZIRCON

Type: Silicate/nesosilicate, zircon, usually free of inclusions.

Colours: Light pastel to deep intense blue with subtle greenish undertones; sometimes heat-treated.

Availability: Relatively common.

Physical benefits: Said to help relieve allergies, particularly connected with breathing, due to air-borne pollen, spores, dust mites or fur, long-term memory loss resulting from trauma or accident, blood clots, strokes; improve eyesight, optical nerve, cataracts, voice loss especially due to stress; be good for healing women over 50 of all problems.

Emotional healing: Blue zircon brings peace of mind where faith has been shaken by betrayal from someone who was deeply trusted; restores self-esteem if the guilty party tried to offload all the blame.

Chakra: Throat.

Candle colour: *Blue.*
Fragrances: *Honey, honeysuckle, hyacinth, lavender, lilac.*
Practical uses: *A traveller's crystal on long journeys, especially to countries where there has been unrest or terrorism; good for discovering the real place and culture; also for successful long-term contracts abroad and emigration or naturalization.*
Magical significance: *Blue zircon is said to lose colour just before a potential crisis, not to predict the inevitable but to advise caution in current projects or dealings with people you do not know well; check small print and information given and all will be fine. The zircon is reflecting your own uncertainties.*
Divinatory meaning: *Look to tried-and-tested information and consult experts in areas of potential dispute or uncertainty.*
Zodiac: *Sagittarius.*
Empowerment: *I draw strength from my ancestors.*

The Roman Pliny the Elder (AD 23–79) compared blue zircon's colour to hyacinths; this name is occasionally applied to blue zircon though it is usually now called starlite in the gem trade. Blue zircon has been prized in jewellery for hundreds of years and was beloved by Victorians as large ornate stones in rings and brooches, notably around the 1880s.

An excellent crystal for connecting with ancestors, researching family origins and visiting ancestral areas. Blue zircon is a wise-woman stone, worn by older women following a spiritual path or those who choose to remain alone after a separation or bereavement.

GREEN APATITE

Type: Apatite is the most common phosphate. Beautiful green apatite comes from the Printzskiold Mine in Malmberget, Sweden.

Colours: Green, yellow-green, yellow, also blue.

Availability: Obtainable through specialist jewellery and crystal stores and online, but rare in yellow.
Physical benefits: May aid brittle bones, growth problems in children, hypertension, heart valves, jaw, metabolism, the absorption of calcium, glands, fluid imbalances, gallbladder and spleen in more yellow shades; autism, Attention Deficit Hyperactivity Disorder and hyperactivity, especially where diet may be implicated.

Emotional healing: Assists with aloofness and alienation, heartbreak in love and inability to move on from love that did not last or develop; yo-yo dieting where bingeing is followed by fasting, bulimia.

Chakra: Heart and Root.

Candle colour: *Green.*
Fragrances: *Basil, bay, fern, moss, rosemary.*
Practical uses: *Plant natural green apatite for success in organic gardening, whether growing flowers, fruit or vegetables, and for relocating realistically from town to country living.*
Magical significance: *Good for increasing psychic and telepathic communication with animals and birds, especially pets and local wildlife, and for animal healing.*
Divinatory meaning: *Open yourself to new friendships and connections to regain your old love of life.*
Zodiac: *Virgo and Libra.*
Empowerment: *The rhythm of life has a powerful pulse.*

The name apatite is derived from the Greek word meaning "to deceive" because varieties of the gem were often confused with other minerals. Called the "bones of the Earth": one of the best crystals for healing the Earth and receiving healing through natural essential oils, herbs and flower essences.

The stone of the crystal healer, green apatite increases receptivity to its healing properties and enhances effects of other crystals.

Keep green apatite near a computer or printer if you send out invitations or invite neighbours for a social event or to join together over an environmental issue.

TREE AGATE

Type: Chalcedony with dendrite inclusions; quite coarse and knobbly even when tumbled.

Colours: White with feathery green tree-like inclusions or veins or, less commonly, green with white tree-like markings.

Availability: Common.

Physical benefits: May clear energy blockages and fluid retention, and absorb pain, especially if placed on a point of pain; said to help vein and capillary problems, neuralgia.

Emotional healing: Brings peace to a troubled mind; heals the pain of unhappy childhood or effects of divorce.

Chakra: Heart.

Candle colour: *Pale green.*
Fragrances: *Cedar, cypress, pine, tea tree.*
Practical uses: *A crystal of abundance if planted with a small tree.*
Magical significance: *Place one on a picture of rainforests to protect them and trees everywhere. Light a green candle and visualize new shoots emerging.*
Divinatory meaning: *Not a time to be alone; seek support and, if in doubt, go back to your spiritual roots for the answer.*
Zodiac: *Virgo.*
Empowerment: *I constantly seek new connections.*

Tree Agate, proper name Dendritic Agate, is named after Dendrite – the old Greek name for a tree and is associated with the Ancient Greek dryads, woodland and tree spirits. Dendritic or tree agate was buried in the fields by the Ancient Greeks at the time of sowing to ensure a good harvest.

Strengthens family connections; use dendritic or tree agate to call estranged family members home by keeping a crystal next to a photograph of the person who has gone away. Protective for travel by air or car.

CHLORITE

Type: Silicate with iron, magnesium and aluminium; often the name given to a group of minerals, but here referring to the green kind.

Colours: Green, occasionally white, yellow, red, lavender or black.

Availability: Rare as separate crystal; more common as inclusions in other crystals.

Physical benefits: Believed to be a whole-body healer, may help with skin surface growths, blemishes, skin tags, assimilation of vitamins and minerals especially A and E, iron, magnesium and calcium, pain relief, deep-seated growths or illnesses that attack or mutate the body's cells or immune system.

Emotional healing: Releases secret sorrows; allows the acutely sensitive and easily wounded to become more emotionally robust.
Chakra: Heart.

Candle colour: *Green.*
Fragrances: *Apple blossom clary sage, cedarwood, rosewood, thyme.*
Practical uses: *Clears away dissension, disharmony, dissolves anger and irritability at home or work; defuses the easily offended, supercritical, sarcastic and tactless who are unaware or uncaring of the effects they have on others.*
Magical significance: *Chlorite is regarded as a very magical stone, showing an inner green land where tiny beings live; use for visualization or guided fantasy shamanic journeys into worlds of magical animals and forests to rediscover your lost inner self.*
Divinatory meaning: *Do not listen to gossip nor pass scandal on as you may become implicated in a secretly growing conflict.*
Zodiac: *Virgo.*
Empowerment: *I seek wisdom within myself.*

Chlorites are most frequently found as strong green inclusions in or coatings on quartz, danburite, topaz, calcite and other minerals. This is the most useful form for healing and everyday purposes. The more rare chlorite phantom quartz is formed when chlorite coating around a quartz crystal is enclosed by further growth by the quartz so the chlorite appears ghost-like within; an excellent other-dimensional exploration tool.

A crystal of vegetarians and vegetarianism and organic food; keep a bowl of chlorite in quartz on the dining table to encourage healthy eating or if you wish to open a wholefood business, store or restaurant.

EPIDOTE QUARTZ/DREAM QUARTZ

Type: Clear quartz with epidote inclusions, either as a green phantom or shadowy inner crystal, or with epidote filling the quartz.

Colours: Light green to bluish green, sometimes with darker markings in the tumblestone.

Availability: Obtainable from specialist mineral stores and online, rarer as tumblestones.

Physical benefits: May help with obesity, glandular fever, Hodgkinson's disease, mumps, fluid retention, kidney stones, recurring viruses and infections, internal parasites; recovery after illness or surgery.

Emotional healing: Brings back hopes after a major setback; good for people whose long-term relationship ends either in unwanted separation or through death.

Chakra: Brow.

Dream quartz blends action-bringing quartz with potential-offering epidote. Carry it to protect you from energy vampires and over-critical or sarcastic people.

At night, write down questions that are troubling you and set the paper under your pillow or by the bed with dream quartz on top. Repeat the questions softer and slower until you drift into sleep. Answers will come in dreams or signs by day. This technique, dream incubation, has been practised since Ancient Egypt.

Wearing or carrying dream quartz makes you intuitive and alert to opportunities and people, acting as a radar to steer you away from bad influences and dead ends.

Candle colour: *Green.*

Fragrances: *Cedarwood, lemongrass, moss.*

Practical uses: *Use dream quartz to take small steps to fulfilment if life is frustrating plans, such as redecorating if you cannot afford to move, having a self-catering holiday if you cannot afford a hotel break.*

Magical significance: *A natural protector against negative energies, human or paranormal, especially at night; encourages beautiful dreams and astral travel to past worlds and to connect with deceased loved ones or guardian angels. Dream quartz will bring the dreams you need and want and assist dream recall.*

Divinatory meaning: *Do not let past failure or present restrictions deter you from future plans, it may just take time.*

Zodiac: *Pisces.*

Empowerment: *I can manifest abundance.*

Actinolite

Type: Amphibole silicate, may be found in quartz.

Colours: Light to rich and dark green, greyish green to black.

Availability: Relatively common.

Physical benefits: Thought to assist the building up of cells and tissues and the regeneration of the body; clear and remove toxins and so assist the healthy functioning of liver and kidneys.

Emotional healing: A "light in the darkness" crystal that counteracts a sense of having lost the way from goals and dreams; helps to prevent loneliness and alienation by opening our heart to others and so creating correspondingly friendly vibes in social encounters (especially lighter and brighter green actinolite).

Chakra: Heart in its green form, Root in black.

Often called ray stone because of its physical structure and the way its energies radiate light throughout the aura, expanding positive connection with others and with the cosmos. Said to promote unity of humankind by spreading goodwill and understanding.

An ideal crystal, especially actinolite in quartz or green actinolite, when travelling to help you tune in to lifestyle and customs of locals; helpful also if you are new in any situation to blend in and understand underlying power structure. After trauma or unwelcome change, actinolite offers a personal sense of security to reach out for new opportunities.

Candle colour: *Bright green.*
Fragrances: *Fennel, fern, grapefruit, lavender, lime, orange.*
Practical uses: *Keep actinolite in any colour in a window if you live in a neighbourhood where there is intolerance or trouble to shield your household from threat or harm.*
Magical significance: *Actinolite in black or dark green is an anti-worry stone. When you are worried, sad or feel unnecessarily guilty, touch your actinolite with your index fingers, name the worry and say, "May this worry/burden be taken from me." Once a month pass a lighted incense stick in any tree fragrance over the actinolite to cleanse it.*
Divinatory meaning: *Look for new contacts, groups and networks that will enable you to meet like-minded people.*
Zodiac: *Scorpio.*
Empowerment: *I open myself to the love of humankind.*

EILAT STONE

Type: Mixture of chrysocolla, malachite, turquoise, sometimes with azurite, silver and copper included.

Colours: Green-blue, turquoise, swirling deep green with blue running through it, precise colour depending on proportion of different minerals.

Availability: Obtainable from specialist crystal stores and online, but it no longer all comes from Israel, its land of origin.

Physical benefits: May aid pain relief, massaged or held close to source of pain (best as natural unpolished and dipped in warm water), sinuses, lung, throat and mouth infections and blockages, fevers, inflammation, bone and tissue regeneration, arthritis, wrists, knees and elbows.

Emotional healing: Gives the wisdom to become complete within the self, the best basis for any relationship; detachment from placating immature adults.

Chakra: Solar Plexus, Heart and Throat.

Associated with the biblical wise King Solomon and his base near the Red Sea, Eilat is highly prized as a stone of wisdom and of authority; it brings success to singers and all who work with words or teach media or communication skills, judges and legal professionals, academics, archaeologists, historians, head teachers or educational administrators, ministers of all religions and diplomats.Wear for safe travel and journeys along old trails or to reconstruct pilgrimage routes of the past and to cities or lands steeped in history, especially those to which you feel strong spiritual affinity.

Candle colour: *Turquoise.*

Fragrances: *Benzoin, copal, frankincense, galbanum, sandalwood.*

Practical uses: *As a powerful energy conductor and stone of loving connections, Eilat stone, worn round the neck or in a pouch, gives older people confidence to use their wisdom and experience in a youth-orientated world, command respect, live happily alone or attract a partner of emotional maturity.*

Magical significance: *Valued as a crystal of formal magic since King Solomon is credited in mystical tradition with the creation of ceremonial magic, planetary and colour associations.*

Divinatory meaning: *Someone is behaving childishly but do not descend to their level; stand back until tantrums end.*

Zodiac: *Sagittarius.*

Empowerment: *Wise thoughts precede my words and deeds.*

Bowenite/New Jade

Type: Very hard antigorite form of serpentine.

Colours: Pale to mid-green.

Availability: Common.

Physical benefits: Said to help with blood sugar, diabetes especially Type 2 levels, hormonal swings especially in pregnancy, flow of milk in mothers who are having problems breast-feeding. Also believed to be good for alopecia in women and hair thinning in men, nails, heart, cholesterol levels, DNA issues, fertility if medical intervention is necessary.

Emotional healing: Overcomes crippling fears of perceived physical danger, such as heights, darkness, elevators and unfamiliar places; helps to make a total break whether from a destructive person or a habit that is damaging health.

Chakra: Heart.

Before the Russian Revolution, bowenite was prized in the Russan imperial court as a crystal that combines strength with beauty. It diminishes the power of a controlling partner or bullying boss or relation, and is the crystal of the warrior in love and life, to show tough love for friends, family or neighbours to help you to say no and leave people to fix their own problems; a good house-buying or -selling crystal, especially if kept with official papers to minimize any legal delays.

Candle colour: *Pale green.*
Fragrances: *Basil, bay, eucalyptus, lemon, lemongrass.*
Practical uses: *Gives confidence to try new activities and so especially good for nervous children to socialize, to answer questions in class and also to stand up to bullying or teasing. Keep a piece with a picture of your child having a good time.*
Magical significance: *Use as a protective love amulet if people interfere in your relationships or a love rival is trying to tempt your partner away.*
Divinatory meaning: *Because you are naturally eager to help, someone close is asking for one too many favours and so not learning to stand on their own feet.*
Zodiac: *Cancer and Aquarius.*
Empowerment: *I can be assertive without being aggressive.*

DEMANTOID GARNET

Type: Andradite garnet, calcium iron silicate. Russian demantoid has golden-brown crystal thread inclusions of chrysotile, called horsetail.

Colours: Deep emerald green(most precious and rarest colour), various shades of green from light green.

Availability: Very rare garnet, highly valuable.

Physical benefits: May help eyesight (second only to emerald in effectiveness), recurring colds, bronchitis, pneumonia, septicaemia, secondary tumours, blocked arteries.

Emotional healing: Reduces loneliness and isolation, especially only children or those away from parents in care.

Chakra: Heart.

This fabulous garnet can be difficult to buy and the most expensive. However, you can obtain rough-cut gems online or pick up demantoid garnets set as antique jewellery. Smudge over an old demantoid with an incense stick in a tree fragrance to make it your own. Often called the star of the garnets, its name means diamond-like because of its brilliance; a stone to pledge that nothing will come between your love. Buy yourself one if alone as a reminder to value yourself highly and demand consideration from others.

Candle Colour: *Green.*

Fragrances: *Cedar, lily, lotus.*

Practical uses: *Wear if you know your insecurities or those of your partner put a strain on relationships. Good for working with a love partner.*

Magical significance: *Demantoid garnet removes obstacles in the way of love. Light a green candle and hold your demantoid. Wait until the wax begins to melt and say, "May his/her heart be softened and turn to me."*

Divinatory meaning: *A stubborn person will come round to your viewpoint if you ask again and then leave it.*

Zodiac: *Aquarius.*

Empowerment: *I do not need to intervene to make things happen.*

VARISCITE

Type: Hydrated aluminium phosphate.

Colours: Light green to apple to bright green, bluish green or turquoise, often with patterned light and darker brown veins across the surface.

Availability: Obtainable through specialist crystal stores and online.

Physical benefits: Said to help strengthen male reproductive system, a crystalline Viagra; improve and maintain health, arteries, veins, blood vessels, nerves.

Emotional healing: Thought to ease fear and worry, relieve stress and depression and increase awareness of the cause of problems; attract new friends.

Chakra: Solar Plexus and Heart.

Variscite is named after the Latin name for Vogtland in Saxony, where its colour matched the costumes of the dancers at the traditional spring festivals that may still be seen today. Flat, polished varieties make excellent worry stones. By holding and stroking them, your anxieties will be reduced. Whenever in a difficult situation, hold the stone, reciting a comforting empowerment in your mind, such as "I feel calm and happy". Variscite will help you settle in a new area or career; good for any pets who are far from their native habitat or natural climate.

Candle colour: *Green.*
Fragrances: *Anise, basil, geranium, jasmine, thyme.*
Practical uses: *Acts as a filter of irritations and outside worries disturbing domestic peace.*
Magical significance: *Pass round a group for focusing healing powers.*
Divinatory meaning: *You may need to draw on your inner resources rather than outside help.*
Zodiac: *Taurus and Gemini.*
Empowerment: *I release my fears and welcome harmony in my mind, my body and my spirit.*

GREEN ZIRCON

Type: Silicate/nesosilicate, zircon.

Colours: Brilliant green, yellowish green, brownish green; can sometimes be cloudy.

Availability: Relatively common.

Physical benefits: May help with lungs, cystic fibrosis; allergies due to pollen and plants, wheat and other grain allergies, heart, heart pacemaker surgery; assist all forms of natural healing especially using herbs and tree essences; good for connective tissue, nerve connectivity, regrowth and restoration of normal body functioning after invasive treatment, transplants and transfusions.

Emotional healing: Reduces emotional dependency on others that can stifle relationships and friendships and over-possessiveness or over-concern with the lives of others.

Chakra: Heart.

Green zircon is the zircon of abundance and growth in every area of life and of creating beauty and harmony even in unpromising situations; good for all personal, home or work makeovers and for creating a good social life if you have got out of the habit.

Wear green zircon to feel prosperous and in doing so to attract prosperity through the growth of income; traditionally worn by those who want a wealthy or beautiful partner: in the modern world wear it to find someone who shares your dreams and will work with you to fulfil them.

Candle colour: *Green.*
Fragrances: *Basil, clary sage, pine, rosemary, thyme.*
Practical uses: *Encourages development of new friendships and revival of those that have ceased through physical distance, a new partner or pressures of work; good for forming social groups based on mutual needs and interest, such as for single parents and children or neighbourhood improvement schemes.*
Magical significance: *One of the most powerful zircon anti-theft and -loss crystals; wear green zircon when travelling, to keep your possessions safe; keep your zircon out of sight when in crowded places (a pendant is ideal).*
Divinatory meaning: *Buy something small and beautiful or make a small improvement to beautify yourself or your home.*
Zodiac: *Virgo and Libra.*
Empowerment: *I make beauty out of ugliness.*

Ruby in Fuchsite

Type: Silicate with corundum inclusions.

Colours: Green with red inclusions.

Availability: Relatively common.

Physical benefits: Recommended by some for carpal tunnel syndrome, repetitive strain injury, immune system, infections, energizing the body, spinal column, red and white blood cell imbalances, heart and restoration of health after a period of feeling unwell.

Emotional healing: Helps to bounce back after emotional upset or tension and deal with situations as they really are, without over-reacting or internalizing the problem and fretting endlessly over it.

Chakra: Heart.

Candle colour: *Green or pink.*
Fragrances: *Basil, bay, cherry blossom, lavender, rose.*
Practical uses: *A stone for adapting to unexpected new circumstances in a long-term relationship, such as a baby when you thought your family was complete; good for the partners of service personnel to adjust to frequent location changes.*
Magical significance: *Use a ruby in fuchsite massage wand as a magic wand to bring lasting love into or back into your life; spiral it in different directions as you call a lover known by name or as yet unknown, faster and faster as you move the wand faster and faster to release the power.*
Divinatory meaning: *You may be passionate about a new person or plan but let matters develop slowly so you can be sure.*
Zodiac: *Aquarius.*
Empowerment: *Each day I grow in a new way.*

Fuchsite is the green chromium-rich variety of muscovite crystals; with inclusions of ruby it becomes very dynamic, even more active than the similar-looking ruby in zoisite. Fuchsite is a stone of nature spirits, earth and air; ruby of love, passion and fire.

These energies together rejuvenate mind, body and spirit, and ruby empowers you to reach out for your heart's desire – giving you motivation and strength.

Wear ruby in fuchsite when coming out of a difficult life change or emotional trauma to regenerate your passion for life and replace what did not work with attainable goals. Take a ruby in fuchsite angel or sphere with you if you are emigrating or going to live in your partner's home country or adopt their religion.

PERIDOT

Type: Silicate/nesosilicate, gemstone variety of olivine.

Colours: Usually bright green, due to its iron content.

Availability: Relatively common.

Physical benefits: Claimed to increase effectiveness of other medications and treatment; may help with ulcers, stings and bites that cause an allergic reaction, asthma, digestive disorders, colon, pancreas, gall bladder, eyesight, gastroenteritis, IBS, Crohn's disease, breasts; assist weight gain; believed to stimulate overdue labour; relieve swellings and growths of all kind.

Emotional healing: Guards against destructive jealousy caused by betrayal in past relationships and personal fears that we are unlovable, rather than relating to the present relationship.

Chakra: Solar Plexus and Heart.

Candle colour: *Olive green.*
Fragrances: *Bay, cedar, juniper, lemon balm, lemon verbena.*
Practical uses: *A wise money crystal: keep with credit cards to spend sensibly. Wear a peridot ring when you go shopping with shopaholics. Good for getting bargains on eBay.*
Magical significance: *Peridot is a magical stone for finding love via the Internet if it is difficult for you to get out and socialize. Hold your peridot jewellery just before opening a friendship or dating site and say, "Wise gem, guide me to good love and protect me from those who would deceive me." Put on the jewellery and follow your instincts.*
Divinatory meaning: *Rely on luck and take a chance on a new offer or opportunity rather than holding back.*
Zodiac: *Taurus and Libra.*
Empowerment: *People respond positively towards me.*

Peridot was used in Ancient Egypt from 1580 BC for jewellery; it was considered a stone of the sun and so very lucky in drawing money, health, success and love. Peridot is naturally protective against envy, gossip and people who deceive you. The Romans wore peridot in gold rings to bring peaceful sleep, and it is effective if you suffer from recurring nightmares about evil spirits, murders or sexual attacks. Peridot, especially set in gold, evokes a positive, helpful response from normally unhelpful people; wear or carry it when approaching faceless officialdom, especially concerning financial or legal matters.

MALACHITE

Type: Copper carbonate.

Colours: Emerald to grass green with black or pale green stripes, bands, swirls or marbling effect.

Availability: Common.

Physical benefits: May help with immune system, arthritis, tumours, torn muscles, broken bones. toothache, gum infections, sinus blockages. Use only externally and work with polished tumbled stones as the dust can be slightly toxic.

Emotional healing: Gives resistance to emotional blackmail and heals emotional abuse, especially from childhood; encourages healthy relationships based on love and not need.

Chakra: Heart.

Candle colour: *Bright green.*
Fragrances: *Cedar, copal, pine, sage.*
Practical uses: *Keep near microwaves in the kitchen and by televisions in living areas.*
Magical significance: *Overcomes fears of flying if you empower the crystal before a trip by holding it and picturing yourself in the wings of Raphael, the archangel.*
Divinatory meaning: *Let go of the past and move forward to what you most desire.*
Zodiac: *Scorpio.*
Empowerment: *I will follow my heart.*

A stone of the most powerful love goddesses, for example our Lady of the Mountains in Central Russia or Freyja the Viking goddess of love and beauty.

Malachite will help you battle against depression or anxiety by encouraging you to uncover the reasons for your distress and then helping you to break negative patterns of behaviour. Speak your fears and sorrows daily aloud as you hold the crystal and then leave your malachite in a sheltered place outdoors overnight to carry away the fears on the winds.

ALEXANDRITE

Type: Rare form of chrysoberyl.

Colours: Rich transparent green.

Availability: Obtainable from specialist crystal stores, high-quality jewellers and online.

Physical benefits: May help spleen, pancreas, testicles, swollen lymph node, Parkinson's disease, Alzheimer's and senile dementia; preserve youthfulness.

Emotional healing: Alexandrite alleviates grief for people lost through death, estrangement, time and distance and for lost opportunities; keep one in the bedroom of bereaved children.

Chakra: Sacral or Heart.

Candle colour: *Green and red bands, or use two candles, one green and one red.*
Fragrances: *Almond blossom, benzoin, bergamot, marigold, sweet marjoram.*
Practical uses: *Keep one in the car to reduce motion sickness.*
Magical significance: *Develops clairvoyant powers. Keep with tarot cards or runes while you are learning the meanings and wear or set on a table while giving readings.*
Divinatory meaning: *Unexpected good luck; enjoy it and do not waste time worrying if it will last.*
Zodiac: *Scorpio or Gemini.*
Empowerment: *I open myself to infinite possibility.*

Alexandrite was first discovered in the Ural Mountains in Russia on the day Tsar Alexander II came of age in 1830. A luck stone, because alexandrite is personal to the owner; dedicate your alexandrite at noon on the day of the full moon and then monthly. Say as you hold it, "Be for me power and protection." Alexandrite is at its most powerful and luck-bringing when the sun shines on it. It protects against jealousy if you or your partner have a jealous ex-lover who causes trouble.

ATLANTISITE

Type: Combination of stitchtite and serpentine.

Colours: Green serpentine with inclusions of pink to purple stichtite.

Availability: Relatively rare, obtainable through specialist mineral stores and online.

Physical benefits: May help with heart, lungs, stomach, kidneys, cramp, menstrual pain and excess or absent flow, hernias, skin complaints and wrinkles, digestion, stomach acidity, diabetes, hypoglycaemia.

Emotional healing: Overcomes insecurity; for overcoming a victim mentality.

Chakra: Solar Plexus.

A crystal for those who live alone, to create a happy welcoming home environment and to enjoy your own time and space. It is called the crystal of inner fire, for atlantisite placed on your solar plexus centre, located in the middle of your upper stomach, draws upwards your Kundalini energy.

  This is the power in the base of your spine that activates your sun solar plexus centre for action and success in the world. Do this for a major business surge or for any time you need an instant power boost to succeed or shine.

Candle colour: *Purple.*
Fragrances: *Bayberry, hibiscus.*
Practical uses: *Set in the place where you and the family relax with purple candles to create a sanctuary of calm.*
Magical significance: *Associated with Atlantis, atlantisite is an ancient wisdom stone that offers access to knowledge of different times to make learning ancient forms of healing easier.*
Divinatory meaning: *Someone from the past will return to your life and connect you with people who can enrich your present world.*
Zodiac: *Leo.*
Empowerment: *I take pleasure in childhood spontaneity.*

BROCHANTITE

Type: Sulphate formed in oxidation zone of copper deposits; closely linked with other copper minerals such as azurite and malachite.

Colours: Emerald green, black-green.

Availability: From specialist crystal stores and online.

Physical benefits: May act against fluid retention, environmental pollutants and illnesses made worse by stressful lifestyle, junk food, additives, excessive stimulants; may help spleen, pancreas, prostate, blood, asthma, emphysema and other chronic lung conditions.

Emotional healing: Helps mean people to be more generous with money and love.

Chakra: Heart.

Candle colour: *Green.*
Fragrances: *Cedar, juniper, rosewood.*
Practical uses: *Helps with day-to-day practical functioning of relationships rather than romance; a piece in the home encourages friendship between family members and a willingness to share attention as well as necessary chores.*
Magical significance: *A bringing-together crystal of the spiritual and material, thoughts and emotions.*
Divinatory meaning: *If someone close is being irritating, let them fix their own problems.*
Zodiac: *Libra.*
Empowerment: *I will let life come to me.*

Brochantite was named in 1824 after the eminent French mineralologist Brochant de Villiers, who is most famous for his involvement in the creation of the geological map of France. A hard-working crystal that builds up goodwill in relationships and the expression of love in deeds. In the workplace it represents fulfilling promises; an energizing crystal at home or work for those who are always saying what they will do but never act. Frequently found as twinned crystals, brochantite attracts people who are like you so you do not feel alone.

PYROMORPHITE

Type: Lead chloro-phosphate, small crystals in clusters.

Colours: Bright green, yellow or brown.

Availability: Relatively common.

Physical benefits: Said to increase personal energy levels, help coeliac disease, IBS and all stomach disorders, chills, cleanse blood; assist assimilation of vitamins and minerals, especially B vitamins; regrowth of health after a long illness; can stimulate resistance to disease.

Emotional healing: Clears the mind of negative energy blocks that prevents participation in life and relationships and experiencing feelings of joy.

Chakra: Heart and Solar Plexus.

Candle colour: *Green.*
Fragrances: *Cedarwood, vervain.*
Practical uses: *Draws money through good luck.*
Magical significance: *A crystal of Mother Earth, gives the ability to connect with nature essences. Keep one in a safe place (as it is toxic if ingested), to attract the blessings of the guardians of the land on which your home is built.*
Divinatory meaning: *Rely on logic not emotion.*
Zodiac: *Aries.*
Empowerment: *I can move forward.*

This crystal will increase the effectiveness of other crystals – therefore it is often used in conjunction with one or more other crystals for healing work. If you work with nature in any way, such as gardening, farming or conservation, pyromorphite will assist you to make the best use of available resources and provide stamina needed for the physical aspect of your work.

WARNING: Toxic, do not use pyromorphite in elixirs, wash hands well after handling and keep out of reach of children and pets.

VERDELITE/GREEN TOURMALINE

Type: Silicate.

Colours: Green, green-blue, green-yellow.

Availability: The darker the green, the more rare and valuable the verdelite.

Physical benefits: May benefit blood sugar disorders, rashes, eczema, scars and birthmarks, irritable bowel syndrome and other chronic bowel diseases.

Emotional healing: Balances male and female energies within both men and women; good for overcoming jealousy and envy in self and others.

Chakra: Heart.

Candle colour: *Green.*
Fragrances: *Apple blossom, peppermint, rosemary.*
Practical uses: *Sportspersons can use this crystal to promote stamina.*
Magical significance: *A stone of protection.*
Divinatory meaning: *Now is the time to be tolerant, particularly relating to a situation involving a man who may be causing difficulties.*
Zodiac: *Libra and Scorpio.*
Empowerment: *I value myself for who I am.*

Verdelite (green tourmaline) was traditionally regarded as a magical stone, because if you apply friction, the crystal polarizes and one end becomes magnetic and will attract small light objects. The other end repels them. For this reason, tourmaline may have become the first magic wand, especially as it forms naturally into wand shapes. Green is the colour of good luck and abundance in all things.

Green tourmaline increases opportunities to earn a second income by turning what was just an interest into a money-spinner.

PREHNITE

Type: Silicate; broken surfaces shine like mother-of-pearl.

Colours: Pale green to yellow-green, also grey, white and colourless.

Availability: Common.

Physical benefits: Believed to increase energy at the same time as calming so aids regeneration after fatigue and for stamina when you cannot rest.

Emotional healing: A crystal of unconditional love: helps during relationship crises not to give up. It also eases worries, especially about health.

Chakra: Solar Plexus and Heart.

Candle colour: *Green or white.*
Fragrances: *Lemon valerian, vanilla, vervain.*
Practical uses: *Prehnite should be carried by anyone who finds it difficult to refuse the requests of others.*
Magical significance: *A stone of prediction, especially with other divinatory practices such as reading the tarot or pendulum.*
Divinatory meaning: *It is time to let go of painful memories that may be holding you back.*
Zodiac: *Virgo.*
Empowerment: *I can say no to unreasonable demands.*

Named for the 18th-century Dutchman Hendrik von Prehn, who discovered it in South Africa, prehnite was regarded as a stone of prophecy and shamanism by indigenous sangomas, medicine men and women.
  Prehnite can be used in meditation to provide protection and stop thoughts wandering. It is a dream crystal: placed under a pillow, it will encourage lucid dreaming. Good, too, for remembering early childhood. Calms hyperactive children or animals and assists children with communication difficulties. Place prehnite in your laptop bag to prevent theft.

ENSTATITE IN DIOPSIDE

Type: Silicate/pyroxene, magnesium silicate.

Colours: Green, yellowish, colourless.

Availability: Obtainable from specialist crystal stores and online.

Physical benefits: Said to help anaemia and blood disorders, bruising, damaged tendons or muscles, short-term memory loss after concussion.

Emotional healing: A stone for those who are afraid of being alone who go from one relationship to the next, constantly seeking someone to fill the inner void, to learn to value themselves and their own company.

Chakra: Heart and Crown.

If you cannot find enstatite with diopside, pure enstatite properties are very similar and tend to predominate even in the combined specimen. Pure enstatite can sometimes be of facet quality or cut into dome-shaped cabochons, which may display a cat's-eye effect. Therefore it is very protective and empowering to wear, particularly if you are fighting any legal matters or dealing with unhelpful officialdom. For healing and empowerment, carry a small piece of natural enstatite in diopside in a pouch, to release harmonizing energies that ensure a constant energy flow.

Candle colour: *Dark green.*
Fragrances: *Cloves, juniper, tea tree.*
Practical uses: *The winner's crystal; place enstatite on top of a competition entry or lottery numbers.*
Magical significance: *Enstatite in diopside can be worn or carried as a symbol of intention if you follow a particular spiritual path.*
Divinatory meaning: *Justice matters more to you than winning, but you can have both, so strive for justice.*
Zodiac: *Aries.*
Empowerment: *I walk in faith and trust, most of all in myself.*

CHRYSOPRASE

Type: Gemstone variety of chalcedony.

Colours: Apple or mint green, occasionally lighter green. The colouration is due to trace amounts of nickel.

Availability: Common.

Physical benefits: May help with ears, eyes, stomach ulcers, liver, gout, skin perforations and infections, heart; powerful detoxifier especially of pollutants in the atmosphere; can relieve side-effects of necessary prolonged medication.

Emotional healing: Green chrysoprase worn as jewellery breathes life into a relationship after a betrayal.

Chakra: Heart.

Keep green chrysoprase out of direct sunlight for prolonged periods to avoid fading, and rehydrate occasionally with wet cotton wool. Excellent for problem-solving and finding new approaches and angles, for anyone in the media, publicity or advertising and for writers of fiction to give both originality and realism. In Eastern Europe, possessing a chrysoprase was traditionally believed to help communication with lizards and other reptiles – it certainly brings a closeness and understanding of nature.

Candle colour: *Mint green.*
Fragrances: *Cedarwood, clary sage.*
Practical uses: *To bring spring into your home at any time of the year; open windows and sprinkle water in which green chrysoprase has been soaked.*
Magical significance: *Keep a piece with tarot cards, runes or other divinatory tools to help you see the unexpected in a reading.*
Divinatory meaning: *A new opportunity could move you out of an impasse.*
Zodiac: *Taurus.*
Empowerment: *I open myself to new beginnings.*

Chrysoltile/Chrysotile

Type: A variety of serpentine, chrysotile contains asbestos so best used as a tumblestone

Colours: Grey and white, brown and white, creamy yellow.

Availability: Found in specialist crystal stores and online.

Physical benefits: Believed to relieve chronic fatigue, throat, lung problems, inflammation within body, multiple sclerosis, veins and arteries, assist blood thinning, skin, tissue regrowth.

Emotional healing: For issues of co-dependency and of problematic control issues with and by loved ones.

Chakra: Root and Throat.

A very earthing stone for times when you are being manipulated towards changes you may not want or you feel others have control over your life; gives you the strength and resourcefulness to make your own plans; good for the period after a separation; hold nightly if you need to move on from a person or situation but are afraid of being alone. Promotes telepathic bonds with people far away; helpful for tracing birth-parents or children given up early in life. **WARNING:** Contains asbestos so do not use in elixirs; do not ingest or breathe in the natural form; keep away from children and pets.

Candle colour: *Grey.*

Associated fragrances: *Lemongrass, lime, mugwort, musk, vetivert*

Practical uses: *Carry in a grey or brown drawstring bag when going out with somone who is mean with money or time or at sharing.*

Magical significance: *Aids psychometry, receiving unknown information about a person or object via psychic touch. Hold a tumblestone in the hand you write with and touch an object belonging to the person or their family with the other hand, asking the questions.*

Divinatory meaning: *Resist pressures to change your mind.*

Zodiac: *Gemini and Capricorn.*

Empowerment: *I control my own life..*

SPIDER JASPER

Type: Silicate, microcrystalline quartz, often with organic matter or other minerals as inclusions.

Colours: Earthy browns with white or dark spider-web markings.

Availability: One of the rarer jaspers.

Physical benefits: May help veins and arteries, blood vessels, brain haemorrhages, nerve connections. Could help chronic fatigue syndrome.

Emotional healing: Frees a person from the manipulation of others and from webs of lies or secrecy surrounding birth or early life; good for escaping from emotional abusers and those who use love as a weapon.

Chakra: Root.

As its name suggests, spider jasper contains the power of the wise spider, represented by the Native North American goddess, Grandmother Spider, who created people from four different-coloured clays as the nations of the earth and led them from the underworld into the open, where Grandfather Sun breathed life into them. Wear or keep spider jasper with you to overcome a fear of spiders or other crawling insects; for uncovering secrets concerning family members or partners being hidden, for whatever reason.

Candle colour: *Brown.*

Fragrances: *Anise, basil, bay, dragon's blood, mugwort, musk.*

Practical uses: *Dishes of spider jasper tumblestones encourage people to mix at parties or family gatherings.*

Magical significance: *One of the best crystals for keeping away bad dreams; attach one to a dreamcatcher and hang it over your bed.*

Divinatory meaning: *Avoid getting caught up in a web of gossip, though this will be hard.*

Zodiac: *Scorpio.*

Empowerment: *We are all part of the same universal family.*

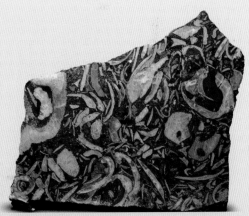

DENDRITIC QUARTZ

Type: Quartz, containing manganese oxide as fern or plant-like black inclusions.

Colours: Clarity varies according to the amount of the inclusion; some quartz can be yellowish or smoky.

Availability: Found in specialist crystal stores and online.

Physical benefits: Said to assist veins, arteries, small capillaries and orifices in the body, nerve connections and endings.

Emotional healing: A crystal for reducing over-dependency on others; for freeing up a co-dependent relationship.

Chakra: Root.

Candle colour: *White.*
Fragrances: *Clematis, ivy, vetivert.*
Practical uses: *Take along to community events or activities at your children's school to find like-minded people.*
Magical significance: *A crystal associated with seasonal celebrations; hold dendritic quartz up to moonlight, press your quartz against the nearest trunk and you will hear psychic messages.*
Divinatory meaning: *You may be feeling claustrophobic in a situation; take a few steps back and gently create your own space rather than walking away.*
Zodiac: *Pisces.*
Empowerment: *I do not need constant company.*

Dendritic quartz is a natural choice to wear or carry if you want to move into the countryside or live by the sea, to open up all kinds of ideas and attract unexpected opportunities. A back-to-nature crystal, hold it in soft sunlight to reconnect with the energies of the natural world and to fill yourself with the life force in its purest form.

   Dendritic quartz opens up children's powers of communication and increases sociability, particularly if they are shy with strangers or do not like being left at nursery or going to school.

CANCRINITE

Type: Felspathoid, sodium calcium aluminium silicate carbonate.

Colours: Yellow, orange, pink, white or blue.

Availability: Obtainable from specialist crystal stores and online.

Physical benefits: Said to help muscles, ligaments, congestion of lungs, pneumonia, bronchitis and chronic breathing difficulties, neck and throat (place directly on/above affected area).

Emotional healing: Reconnects fractured relationships. Chakra: Solar Plexus and Throat.

Cancrinite connects earth and cosmos and draws energies from both, so making it a potent home-blessing stone in all its colours, but especially orange and yellow; makes any social or family occasion harmonious and encourages stimulating communication at mealtimes with a minimum of dramas.

A supportive stone to carry if asking for support or favours and if the outcome of a meeting or application is uncertain, to swing positive energies in your favour.

Candle colour: *Yellow.*

Fragrances: *Chamomile, marigold, sagebrush.*

Practical uses: *Helps resist any form of temptation from spending too much, drinking excessively or straying from a partner.*

Magical significance: *Called the golden healer since it casts a golden shield around the owner's aura energy field.*

Divinatory meaning: *Someone close is worrying; take the time to help resolve it.*

Zodiac: *Aries and Leo,.*

Empowerment: *I walk in the golden light of certainty that I am blessed.*

Shiva Lingham

Type: Crypto-crystalline quartz.

Colours: Variety of earth hues.

Availability: Becoming scarcer, but still available from specialist crystal stores and online.

Physical benefits: Believed to be useful for increasing fertility; relieving impotence and other male sexual dysfunction and premature ejaculation; increasing libido in both sexes; easing childbirth.

Emotional healing: Unites and balances the male and female energies within to create a harmonious whole; good for resolving gender-related issues and for overcoming personal doubts about entering a same-sex relationship.

Chakra: Brow.

Candle colour: *Indigo.*
Fragrances: *Almond, apple, bluebell, orange, rose.*
Practical uses: *If you are still looking for your twin soul, cast a Shiva lingham into a deep lake or on the outgoing tide on New Year's Day or the first day of any month, having breathed on it three times and said, "call my other half to make me complete."*
Magical significance: *Good for sacred or Tantric spiritual sex; for full-moon fertility rituals; leave your Shiva lingham outdoors, if possible in moonlight on the three nights before the full moon. Place it by the bed on the night of the full moon during lovemaking.*
Divinatory meaning: *A turbulent time will pass and new unexpected positive input bring calm to troubled waters.*
Zodiac: Scorpio, the Scorpion.
Empowerment: *I welcome my twin soul into my life.*

In Onkar Mandhata, India, the holy river Narmada flows. In the dry season, a few select locals gather stones named Shiva lingham from the river bed. These are carefully selected and polished by hand to create a potent spiritual talisman now sold all over the world. Shiva lingham is used in the practice of Feng Shui to direct the flow of energies around the home.

Use it to strengthen sexual and loving relationships by placing one or more of these stones in the relationship area of your home (if you are familiar with Feng Shui) or keep a large one in the bedroom and add a smaller on next to it it to conceive a child.

BRIDGE CRYSTAL

Type: A large quartz crystal with a smaller crystal or crystals which is located partially in and partially out of the larger crystal.

Colours: Depends on the quartz.

Availability: Obtainable from specialist crystal stores and online.

Physical benefits: Said to help connections between brain and the body, when another part of the brain takes over from a damaged part, for example after a stroke.

Emotional healing: For a person who has been rejected at an early age and so distrusts relationships.

Chakra: Heart.

A bridge crystal usually has the smaller crystal or crystals at almost a right angle, with the base of the smaller crystal(s) inside the host. Some crystal practitioners regard this as a master or teaching crystal and call it an inner child crystal, particularly if the tip of the small crystal is embedded in the host. Inner-child crystals help undeveloped gifts to emerge, and in rediscovering spontaneity if childhood was traumatic.
   Empower other crystals for healing by placing them next to or resting on the bridge crystal.

Candle colour: *Green.*
Fragrances: *Lavender, lilac.*
Practical uses: *A bridge crystal is the ultimate communication crystal if you live in a multi-cultural area where cultural differences make friendships difficult; take a small bridge with you if you work overseas.*
Magical significance: *Creates mind connections with past worlds and angels.*
Divinatory meaning: *A chance for reconciliation with someone from the past.*
Zodiac: *Gemini.*
Empowerment: *I am open to new ideas.*

ENHYDRO/WATER AGATE

Type: Outer casing of chalcedony within which is sealed a quantity of water. You can hear the water moving if you shake the stone and the water can be seen, if the crystal is held to the light.

Colours: Cloudy white, also in other coloured agates, such as red, grey, dark brown or black or blue.

Availability: Obtainable from a specialist crystals store or online

Physical benefits: Enhydros are a woman's stone; the waters within the crystal reflect her own monthly ebbs and flows, so are believed to benefit hormones and energies; good for relieving PMS, menstrual pain or absence of menstruation.

Emotional healing: One of the most effective stones for healing emotional traumas.

Chakra: Sacral.

Candle colour: *Silver.*
Fragrances: *Jasmine, lemon, lemon balm, lemon verbena, poppy.*
Practical uses: *Helpful around the home for teenagers and pre-pubescent children, especially girls, and for pregnant women and new mothers, to stabilize and channel powerful emotions.*
Magical significance: *Enhydros make men and women more intuitive, telepathic and clairvoyant; use also to connect with your spirit guides and family ancestors.*
Divinatory meaning: *You may be suddenly flooded by the emotions of another person but do not allow this to override your common sense and logic.*
Zodiac: *Cancer.*
Empowerment: *I open myself to my true feelings and desires, and trust my instincts to guide me.*

Representing the waters of the womb of the earth mother, enhydro agate is the stone of Iemanjá, the Yoruba sea goddess, and so a stone both of fertility and abundance. The water in it is said to give access through meditation to the Akashic records or collective well of wisdom. These record the experiences of all people in all places and ages, past, present and future.

Use enhydro or water agate for preserving relationships and situations amid wanted or unwanted change, turbulence and crisis, to enable people to adapt to the new while maintaining and valuing the best of the old.

GROSSULAR GARNET

Type: Silicate, calcium aluminium silicate.

Colours: Colourless, white, pink, cream, orange, red, honey, black or green.

Availability: Found in specialist stores and online.

Physical benefits: Said to be good for the immune system, heart, respiratory system, blood, vitamin deficiency, reproductive problems, deep vein thrombosis (carry green when on a long-haul trip); protect against highly infectious diseases.

Emotional healing: Reduces extremes of emotions; helpful if all your previous relationships have been a drama.

Chakra: Heart.

Candle colour: *White or green.*
Fragrances: *Juniper, rosemary, rue, sandalwood, vervain.*
Practical uses: *Injects romance and fun into an over-practical life and boosts passion and fresh energies into a love weighed down by worry.*
Magical significance: *Red or orange grossular is particularly protective against abusive neighbours or physical threats as it acts as an absorbing shield and reflects back nastiness.*
Divinatory meaning: *Value yourself more highly.*
Zodiac: *Capricorn and Aquarius.*
Empowerment: *I do not need the praise of others to feel worthwhile.*

A stone of strength, grossular garnet will benefit new business ventures. Have a display of small pieces in different colours: clear to boost the initial phase and keep new ideas and customers coming in; green for good luck, continuing growth and warm client contact; orange for ingenuity and creative ideas and advertising; red for stamina and determination.

Grossular garnet is particularly useful for companies offering spiritual products or services to maintain the right atmosphere and ethos but at the same time to make the necessary profit to be viable.

OCEAN JASPER

Type: Orbicular jasper describes several jaspers displaying perfect circles throughout the crystals.

Colours: Multiple colours of green, red, orange, yellow, cream, pink, white and brown with orb-like inclusions.

Availability: Ocean jasper is quite rare but obtainable from some specialist mineral stores and online.

Physical benefits: Claimed to be good for the digestive system; remove toxins that cause body odour and flatulence; help to ease problems with the thyroid, seasickness and inner-ear disturbances.

Emotional healing: Gentle and gradual release of pent-up anger or emotional blockages.

Chakra: Heart.

Candle colour: *White or silver.*
Fragrances: *Galbanum, lavender, lemon.*
Practical uses: *Makes us more patient of ourselves and of others.*
Magical significance: *Use a polished ocean jasper sphere for meditation by soft silver candlelight or moonlight; it is sometimes called the moon gem because of its resemblance to the moon's surface.*
Divinatory meaning: *You will have to take some responsibility for a course of action that involves others.*
Zodiac: *Cancer and Pisces.*
Empowerment: *I flow with my inner tides.*

Ocean jasper is occasionally called orbicular jasper in reference to the orb or bull's-eye patterns that can occur which are also seen in leopardskin and poppy jaspers. The name ocean jasper was given to those orbicular jaspers that can be collected on a remote shore of Madagascar only at low tide as the rest of the time the ocean conceals them.

Ocean jasper is full of positive gentle nurturing energy that helps anyone who wears or holds it regularly to develop self-love and empathy for others.

MUSCOVITE/STAR CRYSTAL

Type: Mica; when its twin yellow variety from Brazil forms a five-pointed star it is called star crystal.

Colours: White, silver, yellow, green (deep green as fuchsite) and brown, often white tinged with other colours; occasionally red or pink to purple.

Availability: Muscovite is common, star muscovite rare.

Physical benefits: Seen as helpful for pancreas, kidneys, allergies, insomnia, blood sugar levels and diabetes.

Emotional healing: Lessens self-doubt and insecurities. Promotes connections with a significant other.

Chakra: Heart.

Muscovite, originally used for window glass, especially in sacred buildings, increases fast thinking and problem-solving skills; use as a good-luck charm for exams, interviews and quizzes. Keep muscovite with study material when learning foreign languages or mastering technical material with whose terms you are unfamiliar. Good for studying spirituality and healing, especially traditional wisdom from Native North America, India or China. Purple muscovite allows contact with higher spiritual planes.

Candle colour: *White.*

Fragrances: *Carnation, copal, galbanum, orange.*

Practical uses: *Reveals lies or exaggeration; set near computers for Internet dating or in a pouch when shopping for goods or services.*

Magical significance: *Use to enhance scrying visions (looking for images in a reflective surface such as crystal or water), held in the hand you do not write with.*

Divinatory meaning: *You may be experiencing strong intuitive thoughts and feelings about a person. Trust these.*

Zodiac: *Leo.*

Empowerment: *I make bridges between people and cultures.*

RUSSIAN RAINBOW PYRITES

Type: Iron sulphide.

Colours: Metallic, darker grey/black with a drusy covering of miniature minerals on the surface, which shimmers with rainbow colours including gold, green, rose pink and blue.

Availability: Relatively rare but very beautiful and so worth obtaining.

Physical benefits: Believed to hellp with migraines with visual disturbances, brain disorders that cause degeneration of the whole body, auto-immune diseases, Huntington's chorea and genetic conditions, colds, influenza and other viral attacks, digestion.

Emotional healing: A very potent stone for adults who have communication difficulties and miss social signals, and so find it hard to make relationships or keep friends; good for adults with Asperger's syndrome.

Chakra: Solar Plexus.

Candle colour: *Silver.*
Fragrances: *Basil, dragon's blood, garlic, ginger.*
Practical uses: *Rainbow iron pyrites brings positive recognition in talent contests, televised quizzes or game shows; should be placed with applications for a few hours before sending to win a place in a reality-TV production.*
Magical significance: *Rainbow pyrite is a welcome addition to ghost investigation, especially in polished form; set one on a table or the floor in a haunted room to attract spirits to manifest and protect from any that are not friendly.*
Divinatory meaning: *Try a new interest or activity that may seem difficult or even a little risky; you will really enjoy it and are braver than you realize.*
Zodiac: *Aries.*
Empowerment: *I will enjoy new activities.*

Like many rainbow crystals, rainbow pyrites, newly discovered near Ulianovsk on the Volga River in Russia, is acquiring myths about being treasure left by earth or water spirits or having fallen from the rainbow. It is considered a good-luck stone, potent for making wishes when there is a rainbow or, even better, a double rainbow. Use it to generate enthusiasm at a dull or cliquey party. Give a piece to young travellers alone, particularly if camping or participating in water sports such as white-water rafting, to keep them safe.
   WARNING: Do not use in elixirs or ingest.

RAINBOW QUARTZ

Type: Silicate/tectosilicate, clear quartz with prismatic fractures within the crystal.

Colours: Light refracted by the prismatic effect of the inclusion.

Availability: Relatively common.

Physical benefits: Thought to be good for bladder, cystitis, kidneys, bowel disorders, constipation, exhaustion, menstrual difficulties, metabolism, Seasonal Affective Disorder.

Emotional healing: Rainbow quartz overcomes deep disappointments and disillusion over the way love, career, family or life turned out: brings the optimism to try again

Chakra: Brow and Crown.

Rainbow quartz combines the dynamic power of clear quartz with the mystical rainbow energies associated with reconciliation and the promises of a better tomorrow. The rainbow amplifies the power of white light into different forms to offer courage and confidence in red, creativity in orange, logic and entrepreneurial qualities in yellow, love and luck in green, career and justice in blue, spiritual powers and imagination in indigo and the ability to make a huge life leap in violet.

Candle colour: *White.*
Fragrances: *Copal, frankincense, lemon, orange, sandalwood.*
Practical uses: *One of the best crystals if you are shy or lacking confidence at social occasions.*
Magical significance: *Rainbow quartz spheres are the perfect divinatory tool for the beginner to see images within.*
Divinatory meaning: *This is a time when lady luck smiles on you.*
Zodiac: *Cancer and Leo.*
Empowerment: *I am optimistic about the future.*

INDEX

Relationship Issues List

AILMENT	LOVE CRYSTAL
abuse of any kind	fire opal p.39, golden/yellow calcite p.45, malachite p.103, spider jasper p.113
acceptance	aegerine p.68, lilac kunzite p.77
adversity	black tiger's eye p.74
anger	black tiger's eye p.74, blue crystals p.10, chlorite p.93, ocean jasper p.120, red calcite p.36, red carnelian p.35
anxiety	covellite p.80, grossular garnet p.119, keyiapo stone p.46, malachite p.103, orange carnelian p.40, prehnite p.109, schalenblende p.48, smoky quartz p.50, variscite p.99, zincite p.37
assertiveness	bowenite/new jade p.97, red carnelian p.35
balance	clear fluorite p.56
betrayal	blue zircon p.90, chrysoprase p.111, peridot p.102
body-image	aegerine p.68, benitoite p.86, golden/yellow calcite p.45
bullying	bowenite/new jade p.97, red calcite p.36, red jasper p.31
business ventures	grossular garnet p.119
calm	amethyst p.19, atlantisite p.105, black star diopside p.67, blue coral p.79, blue kyanite p.82, blue lace agate p.78, blue quartz p.81, blue sapphire p.89, brecciated jasper p.32, limonite p.42, rainbow moonstone p.54, strawberry quartz p.24
commitment issues	blue sapphire p.89, pink kunzite p.26, shattuckite p.83
communication	blue barite p.87, blue fluorite p.88, blue lace agate p.78, bridge crystal p.117, cancrinite p.115, chrysoberyl p.44, dendritic quartz p.114, prehnite p.109, Russian rainbow pyrites p.122, window quartz p.53
confidence	bowenite/new jade p.97, brecciated jasper p.32, carnelian p.21, jewellery p.7, p.15, keyiapo stone p.46, Russian quartz p.123
controlling behaviour	bowenite/new jade p.97, golden/yellow calcite p.45, iron pyrites p.65, red calcite p.36, stibnite p.63, strawberry quartz p.24
courage	benitoite p.86, carnelian p.21, fire opal p.39, orange carnelian p.40, red carnelian p.35, red jasper p.31
creativity	black star diopside p.67, bryozoan p.59, fire opal p.39, zincite p.37
criticism	chlorite p.93, epidote/dream quartz p.94, iron pyrites p.65, strawberry quartz p.24
danger/accident prevention	anthracite p.60, meteorite p.62
deceit	bixbite p.33, lemon chrysoprase p.43, peridot p.102, sphalerite p.73
dependency	dendritic quartz p.114, green zircon p.100
depression	aegerine p.68, Botswana agate p.25, covellite p.80, jet p.72, malachite p.103, sphalerite p.73, variscite p.99
destructive relationships	bowenite/new jade p.97, golden/yellow calcite p.45
diplomacy	franklinite p.49
disagreements	schalenblende p.48
disappointment	rainbow quartz p.123
domineering behaviour	brecciated jasper p.32
dreams	black kyanite p.70, brecciated jasper p.32, epidote/dream quartz p.94, larvakite p.76, prehnite p.109, rainbow moonstone p.54, ruby p.34, turritella agate p.47
eating disorders	green apatite p.91, orange carnelian p.40
emotional blocks	blue barite p.87, clear fluorite p.56, franklinite p.49, halite p.28, ocean jasper p.120, smoky quartz p.50, wulfenite p.41
emotional healing	apophyllite p.52, enhydro/water agate p.118, rainbow moonstone p.54
emotional pressure/ manipulation	blue kyanite p.82, bryozoan p.59, jewellery p.7, lemon chrysoprase p.43, malachite p.103, spider jasper p.113
empathy	ocean jasper p.120
energy/stamina	aegerine p.68, brecciated jasper p.32, grossular garnet p.119, healer's gold p.75, pyromorphite p.107, smoky quartz p.50, sphalerite p.73, verdelite/green tourmaline p.108
faith in others	banded onyx p.55
family connections	chrysoltile p.112, ruby p.34, tree agate p.92, turritella agate p.47
family relationships	apophyllite p.52
fear	anthracite p.60, bowenite/new jade p.97, falcon/hawk's eye p.84, jet p.72, pink topaz p.30, ruby p.34, variscite p.99, zincite p.37

fertility	amber p.21, black coral p.69, Botswana agate p.25, bowenite/new jade p.97, keyiapo stone p.46, orange carnelian p.40, pink topaz p.30, red jasper p.31, schalenblende p.48, Shiva lingham p.116, silver p.64, turritella agate p.47
fidelity	blue sapphire p.89, healer's gold p.75, jet p.72
friendship/social matters	actinolite p.95, benitoite p.86, blue kyanite p.82, bridge crystal p.117, brochantite p.106, clear danburite p.57, copper nugget p.38, dendritic quartz p.114, golden/yellow calcite p.45, green zircon p.100, Russian quartz p.123, Russian rainbow pyrites p.122, schalenblende p.48, spider jasper p.113, variscite p.99
generosity	brochantite p.106, chrysoltile p.112
gentle love	rhodonite p.27
grief	alexandrite p.104, bixbite p.33, black coral p.69, black star diopside p.67, black tiger's eye p.74, Botswana agate p.25, dinosaur bone p.51, galena p.66, healer's gold p.75, jet p.72, smoky quartz p.50
grounding	franklinite p.49, larvakite p.76, limonite p.42, melanite garnet p.71, sphalerite p.73
guilt	aegerine p.68, blue kyanite p.82, brecciated jasper p.32, melanite garnet p.71, wulfenite p.41
healing	blue sapphire p.89, franklinite p.49, green apatite p.91, stibnite p.63, turritella agate p.47
heartbreak	aegerine p.68, bixbite p.33, green apatite p.91, pink kunzite p.26
home	actinolite p.95, anthracite p.60, apophyllite p.52, black coral p.69, blue barite p.87, bowenite/ new jade p.97, cancrinite p.115, chiastolite p.61, copper nugget p.38, dinosaur bone p.51, lemon chrysoprase p.43, limonite p.42, meteorite p.62, rainbow moonstone p.54, silver p.64, smoky quartz p.50, zincite p.37
honesty	lemon chrysoprase p.43
independence	chrysoltile p.112, sphalerite p.73
insecurity	atlantisite p.105, demantoid garnet p.98, muscovite/star crystal p.121
insomnia	aegerine p.68, pink kunzite p.26, smoky quartz p.50, stilbite p.29
jealousy	aegerine p.68, alexandrite p.104, falcon/hawk's eye p.84, golden/yellow calcite p.45, jet p.72, lemon chrysoprase p.43, peridot p.102, red carnelian p.35, verdelite/green tourmaline p.108
leadership	chrysoberyl p.44

lone parents	red jasper p.31
loneliness	demantoid garnet p.98, enstatite in diopside p.110
loss	bixbite p.33, black coral p.69, black tiger's eye p.74, bryozoan p.59, galena p.66, jet p.72, stilbite p.29
love	healer's gold p.75, jade p.21, pink kunzite p.26, silver p.64
loyalty	bixbite p.33
luck	alexandrite p.104, aventurine p.21, banded onyx p.55, black coral p.69, blue sapphire p.89, copper nugget p.38, healer's gold p.75, muscovite/star crystal p.121, red carnelian p.35, Russian rainbow pyrites p.122, schalenblende p.48, silver p.64, smoky quartz p.50, verdelite/green tourmaline p.108
lying	falcon/hawk's eye p.84, lemon chrysoprase p.43, muscovite/star crystal p.121, pink topaz p.30, ruby p.34, spider jasper p.113
male potency	black coral p.69, melanite garnet p.71, variscite p.99
manipulative behaviour	bixbite p.33, brecciated jasper p.32, chrysoltile p.112, iron pyrites p.65, spider jasper p.113, stibnite p.63
mood	halite p.28, rainbow moonstone p.54
negativity	black coral p.69, black kyanite p.70, clear danburite p.57, clear fluorite p.56, jet p.72, limonite p.42, wulfenite p.41
neighbours	brecciated jasper p.32, chrysocolla p.85, limonite p.42
nightmares	brecciated jasper p.32, peridot p.102, ruby p.34, spider jasper p.113, stilbite p.29
panic attacks	black kyanite p.70, Botswana agate p.25, red calcite p.36, smoky quartz p.50
parent, loss of	bryozoan p.59, stilbite p.29
patience	ocean jasper p.120
phobias	Botswana agate p.25, turritella agate p.47
possessiveness	blue kyanite p.82, green zircon p.100, red carnelian p.35
prosperity/financial matters	anthracite p.60, apophyllite p.52, chrysoberyl p.44, copper nugget p.38, fire opal p.39, franklinite p.49, green zircon p.100, iron pyrites p.65, jet p.72, jewellery p.7, larvakite p.76, peridot p.102, red carnelian p.35, schalenblende p.48, silver p.64, stibnite p.63, verdelite/green tourmaline p.108
psychological attacks	jewellery p.7, ruby p.34

rationality	larvakite p.76
reconciliation	bixbite p.33, cancrinite p.115, chrysoprase p.111, franklinite p.49, rainbow quartz p.123
relationship breakdown	dinosaur bone p.51, epidote/dream quartz p.94, galena p.66, lilac kunzite p.77, pink kunzite p.26, rhodonite p.27, schalenblende p.48, shattuckite p.83, stilbite p.29
resentment	golden/yellow calcite p.45, lemon chrysoprase p.43, wulfenite p.41
revitalizing relationships	orange carnelian p.40
secrecy	spider jasper p.113
self-belief	benitoite p.86
self-consciousness	aegerine p.68
self-destructive behaviour	chiastolite p.61, window quartz p.53
self-doubt	brecciated jasper p.32, muscovite/star crystal p.121, strawberry quartz p.24
self-esteem	blue zircon p.90, golden/yellow calcite p.45, strawberry quartz p.24
self-harming	rainbow moonstone p.54, red calcite p.36, smoky quartz p.50
self-limiting behaviour	falcon/hawk's eye p.84
sensitivity	Botswana agate p.25, chlorite p.93
separation	twin/Gemini quartz p.58
sex, indiscriminate	red calcite p.36, sphalerite p.73
sexual desire	bixbite p.33, fire opal p.39, red calcite p.36, red carnelian p.35, ruby p.34
stubbornness	black star diopside p.67
team building	aegerine p.68, schalenblende p.48
training	golden/yellow calcite p.45, larvakite p.76
travel	actinolite p.95, aegerine p.68, blue coral p.79, blue zircon p.90, chiastolite p.61, falcon/hawk's eye p.84, green zircon p.100, Russian rainbow pyrites p.122, silver p.64, tree agate p.92, turritella agate p.47
trust	blue sapphire p.89, bridge crystal p.117, pink topaz p.30
truth	blue fluorite p.88, blue sapphire p.89, sphalerite p.73, stibnite p.63
undesirable influences	schalenblende p.48
unrequited love	lemon chrysoprase p.43, pink topaz p.30, rhodonite p.27

vaginismus	orange carnelian p.40
victim mentality	atlantisite p.105, turritella agate p.47
violence	chrysocolla p.85, red jasper p.31, rhodonite p.27
wisdom	blue sapphire p.89, dinosaur bone p.51, Eilat stone p.96, enhydro/water agate p.118, meteorite p.62, turritella agate p.47
workplace	flower jasper p.15, rainbow moonstone p.54, twin/Gemini quartz p.58

CREDITS